# Psalms for Living

E M Blaiklock

Commentary on the Psalms

Volume 1

# Psalms for Living

Psalms 1-72

Scripture Union

47 Marylebone Lane, London W1M 6AX

First published 1977

ISBN 0 85421 520 4



Designed by Tony Cantale

Printed by Hazell Watson & Viney Ltd, Aylesbury, Bucks

## Publisher's Introduction

The book of Psalms surely needs little introduction to the Christian reader. The hymnbook of the Jewish Temple, it has from the very first been an important part of the Christian heritage. The quality of their poetry, the majestic grandeur of their vision of the Creator-God, their perceptive insights into human nature and their simple piety have made them an indispensable part of both public worship and private devotion. Joy and sorrow, trust and doubt, success and failure, hope and despair – all human experience is reflected here and each of us can readily identify with the struggles and sentiments of the original writers. Their profound statements about man's relationship with God and with his fellows speak with a renewed potency and relevancy to every age. It is this that Professor Blaiklock helps us to see in these pages. Each psalm is firmly placed in its original setting in an introductory paragraph, and verse by verse comments bring out the abiding relevance and contemporary significance.

These books have been designed primarily as a devotional commentary, but their content and layout will make them the ideal basis for a daily reading programme. Most psalms are of a suitable length for this purpose and others will easily subdivide. Readers will probably find that the RSV is the most useful version but Professor Blaiklock has used a wide variety of translations, some of which are designated by the abbreviations listed below.

## Abbreviations

| | |
|---|---|
| AAT | An American Translation, Smith and Goodspeed |
| JB | Jerusalem Bible |
| KJV | Authorised (King James) Version |
| LB | The Living Bible |
| NASB | New American Standard Bible |
| NEB | New English Bible |
| RSV | Revised Standard Version |
| RV | English Revised Version |
| LXX | Septuagint (Greek Version of the Old Testament) |

## Author's Preface

The Psalter is a book of prayers rather than a prayer book. Its words leap to the page from the heart of man, racked by pain, jubilant with joy, despairing, aspiring, questioning, worshipping, but never ceasing to reach for God.

The world changes, knowledge grows, but the heart of man remains as it has always been. That is why the psalms become increasingly, as life goes on, the mirror and the language of experience, the book which speaks to us, and provides the words for the hours of contrition, of fear, of awe, defeat and victory.

And that is why each reader of the psalms could write his own commentary. This book is as the writer's life has made it. It is called a devotional commentary in the hope that, like the psalms themselves, it may add meaning to some reader's experience and sharpen the relevance of words already immortal.

The psalms are poetry and, like all poetry, have meaning which varies with the mood, the perplexity or the passion which each one who reads them brings to his reading. What strikes home to one may pass another by. When any commentator can comment on great poetry with cold detachment, he has lost the ability to comment. On the other hand a poem may mean to a reader more than the poet first intended. This perhaps is the test of true poetry, and especially of the poetry of the Bible, in which God's Spirit had a part.

Here, then, with what elucidation one man's mind and life's experience may bring, is a book about the psalms. The paths man treads are trodden well and their rough places and their plain are old familiar ground. A guide can sometimes help, and a guidebook, imperfect, no doubt, and certainly incomplete, is the book which follows.

E. M. Blaiklock

Titirangi
Auckland N.Z.

**Read Psalms 1.1,2; 119.1–8**

### Occasion and author

No author can be ascribed to this psalm. It could be the work of the anthologist who collected the sayings on the Word, which make up the longest of the psalms – Psa. 119. If conjecture may be pressed a little further, it is possible to form a picture of a devout Jew who had known the pain, the humiliation, and the hopes and fears of exile, who put into Book V several minor collections of psalms, including his own anthology, and then, called to play a major part in the editing of the Psalter, wrote the first psalm in the book as an introduction.

It may have been the Exile, when all else was lost, which drove a suffering people to put their 'songs of Zion' (137.3) together and to add to them. Here was emotion, recollected, not 'in tranquillity', as Wordsworth's well-known definition of poetry would have it, but in pain, turmoil of spirit and desperation. Perhaps a shadowy figure emerges as we read Psa.1 and related passages, a devout man washed with sorrow, and tried in his faith, who was a moving spirit in the collection of the psalms.

Like many other ancient writers, Christian and pagan (Luke and Thucydides, John, Paul and Lucretius are examples) the writer began with an elaborately patterned verse. The writer asked the question: 'Who is truly happy?' and answered it in a threefold web of words. Hebrew poetry, by its very parallelism of ideas, can add new dimensions of meaning. In the introduction to this psalm the writer has expended all his art by a parallelism of three times three, which is at the same time a climax. He was a man who sought to give his best to God.

### Commentary

**1** Who then is happy? 'He is a happy man who never allows his course of life to be dictated by those who take no thought of God.' 'Walking', in both Hebrew and Greek, is a metaphor for the pursuit of the various activities of life (John 7.1). The true man of God must, if he is to keep his heart's integrity, the first requisite of happiness, again and again resist public opinion, and reject the trends and fashions of his time. 'Wisdom, domestic calm, and the approval of one's fellows,' said Inge once, are the ingredients of happiness. The Dean stumbled. Wisdom, perhaps as often as not, must disregard the opinion of one's fellows. Let it rather be the approval of one's God. The cheers of the multitude can be too dearly bought, and there is nothing more fickle. Read Browning's poem *The Patriot* and compare Mark 11.9,10 with Mark 15.12,13.

But the answer continues, psychologically apt. Dr. Jekyll, in R. L. Stevenson's macabre story, chose, at first, to become Mr. Hyde. Then the change became involuntary, until the evil personality, hidden but alive in the kindly doctor, took over and triumphed. The writer works it out in his cube:

*walk stand sit*
*counsel way seat*
*ungodly sinners scornful.*

The processes progress, but overlap and interlock. It is quite certain that evil tolerated becomes evil enjoyed. As Pope put it in his *Essay on Man:*

*Vice is a monster of so frightful mien*
*As to be hated needs but to be seen;*
*Yet seen too oft, familiar with her face,*
*We first endure, then pity, then embrace.*

That is exactly what v. 1 means. Who is happy? . . . 'He who does not find his pleasure in the company of those who care nothing for God's laws . . . He who does not adopt the way of life of those who hold God in open contempt.' Samson 'eyeless in Gaza, at the mill with slaves', is a vivid illustration; Samson, splendid to look at, witty, popular, who might even have won the Philistines from the worship of their grotesque deity to a pure faith in Jehovah; Samson, the fool with women, who was seduced by the brilliance of the society of the men from Crete, whose art can be seen at Knossos, their crinolined women, their cruel bull-fighting . . .

**2** But the writer turns from his negatives to a more positive definition. Who is happy? 'The man who in his whole manner of life seeks to do God's will, who is alert for God's guidance and loyal in the rush of the day and the silence of the night . . .' Look at Acts 4.23. Life holds us, society surrounds us, duties press, a godless world calls for this, demands that. The test comes when we are free to choose. Whose company is preferable? Samson was charmed with the enemy. Esther and Mordecai knew what they desired. So, in contrary fashion, did Nehemiah and Ezra. A deep and solemn test is involved. Look searchingly at 1 John 3.13.

And so the question finds its answer. The psalms, like the ministry of Christ, begin with an affirmation: 'Blessed is he . . .' and the conclusion is one to which all honest thought is driven. Consider Coleridge: 'Happiness can be built only on virtue, and must of necessity have truth for its foundation'; and Pascal: 'Happiness is the union of ourselves with God'; and Fichte thoughtfully: 'Happiness is not the purpose of our lives, but to deserve happiness.'

**Read Psalm 1.3–6; Jeremiah 17.5–8**

**3** There could be a link between the writer of the psalm and Jeremiah, for Jeremiah takes up and develops the image of the tree. It 'reaches its roots to the water,' says the prophet, suggesting a conscious seeking for blessing, and that happy alliance of faith and grace which is the very heart of spiritual experience.

The verb is properly 'transplanted' as though the good man is set by the Divine Forester in the place of blessing and usefulness. John 15.16 says as much: 'I have *placed* you so that you may bear fruit.' It is a rich image. It speaks of steadfastness. In these hills where I write are a few remaining specimens of that monarch of the forest, the kauri, so ravaged by New Zealand's pioneers. When a nor'easter blows hard against the ranges, the saplings bend, the twigs and dead leaves fly down the blast, the moving mass of air roars and whistles in the tossing branches – but place the two palms of the hands against the great bole of the tree, and the immobile strength of the trunk may be felt. There is never a tremor, never a quiver. As J.B. Phillips renders Eph. 6.13 – '. . . that even when you have fought to a standstill you may still stand your ground', so is the Christian called upon to confront the thrust and power of a hostile world, firm as the deeply rooted tree.

The tree conserves. They tame the desert, they check and contain erosion. Along the watercourses they hold the bank, grip and conserve the precious topsoil and rebuild it with their fallen leaves. Asia Minor is struggling back to its ancient fertility as the river valleys are filled again with trees. Israel plants trees in millions. North African communities press into the Sahara with trees, trees, trees. The green leaves replenish oxygen, give off moisture to build the beneficent clouds, provide blessed shade. To destroy trees is to prepare the way for the world's death.

So it is with Christian men. 'It is only Christian men,' said G. K. Chesterton in his magnificent *Ballad of the White Horse*, 'guard even heathen things.' And it was never more true that the presence of believing Christians, alive with their faith, their hope, their love, is all that conserves society. Let but the level of a Christian presence fall below a certain point, and violence gathers, cruelty is loose, vice swells and pollutes, and a land decays. There is erosion, pollution and decay of more sorts than that which poisons and rots the physical environment.

**4** The chaff stands in complete contrast with the tree – unstable, dead, useless, harmful. The chaff was a common pest at threshing time, blown on the wind from the high threshing-floors, filling the air, stinging the eyes, for the chaff of the Bible is not the cut straw of the draught-horse's nosebag, familiar sight of the almost forgotten years. It was the broken husks, the stubble, the waste of the harvesting process, fuel for the chance fire and unsalvaged. Isaiah used the image of this psalm five times, and perhaps provided inspiration. It is the 'speck' of the New Testament (Matt. 7.3), dimming the vision.

It is a vivid image. The chaff is separated from the corn, as the wheat is from the tares, by the wind of persecution, by the breath of crisis, by the gale of the ultimate Judgement Day. The world is full of such death, and it is part of the pain of good men to stand in daily contact with that which harms and offends.

**5** If the guess is near the truth, thus stood the writer in Babylon. Perhaps he knew the bullying crowd of Psa. 137, daunted only by the dark words of the commination which closes that sombre little song, and sung by the Jews only as a last defence, as the threatening mob closed in on their riverside meeting place. Some day, somewhere, the writer hopes 'the wicked will cease from troubling . . .'

**6** The two roads in fact will part. The multitude moves on but God marks the righteous feet amid the moving, mingled mass. There is a way of life and a way of death – 'and the choice goes by for ever', as James Russell Lowell put it, 'twixt that darkness and that light'.

**Conclusion**

So ends the psalm. It has a fine unity. It speaks of the two species of men, and follows through to the logic of final separation. In some ancient manuscripts it was not a numbered psalm, Psa. 2 being quoted as Psa. 1 in one of the most authoritative ancient texts (Codex Bezae in Acts 13.33). This is what led to the mistake of Albertus Magnus, the medieval scholar of seven centuries ago (1200–1280), who saw the first two psalms as one, 'beginning and ending in a beatitude'. The style and the theme are visibly different, and some pondering over the anthology of Psa. 119, will reinforce the guess that the introduction came from a great editor's hand, a man who loved the Word.

**Read Psalm 2.1–5; 2 Samuel 15.1–4**

**Occasion and author**

The second psalm plunges into confusion and war. But which war, which tumult? The guesses are almost as numerous as the commentators, but there is an argument which has substance. It may be profitably asked what the original editor thought, and why he placed it second in the Psalter. If indeed he was a devout and learned man, who saw significance in the history of his people, he may have been led from a personal experience of exile to turn, in choice of his first psalms, to the traumatic experience of David in flight before Absalom. He discovered a psalm with a firm tradition attached to it – Psa. 3. A perceptive mind might easily conclude that Psa. 3 came, not at the beginning of the rebellion, but, as the tradition had it, when the retreat to the wilderness was in full train. In ordering the collection, the editor might very naturally conclude that Psa. 2 was the record of an earlier mood, the moment of horror when David, too long at ease, and unaware of the emerging rebellion, was startled into action by realization of wide disaffection, and the peril on the frontiers of his small empire, which trouble in the land would undoubtedly provoke and stimulate.

The early Christians, to be sure, saw messianic prophecy in the psalm (Acts 4.25–27). It is of the nature of prophecy to take its origin and first significance in some smaller context of contemporary events, and to assume widening meaning in the expanding area of history. The psalm has acquired relevance and reality in more than one century, and the vivid application seen by the small embattled group in Jerusalem may appear again in final and deadlier form with the Apocalyptic wars of the Antichrist waged against the royal Messiah and His Church. All prophecy has multiple application in widening circles, as Rev. 13 bears witness. The Beast was the 'divine' emperor calling for the allegiance of men's souls. But such creatures strew history, for 'even now there are many antichrists' (1 John 2.18), and the horrific vision could have international fulfilment, the shape of which can sometimes be foreseen. So with this stormy little poem, ringing with defiance and hope.

**Commentary**

**1** It is a question of horror and sudden stinging awareness. Absalom's revolt was a sordid enough intrigue, and could have reached the disastrous proportions of nationwide disaffection only on the assumption that David had lost touch with affairs. He was culpably indulgent towards the handsome son, born of the foreign woman whom David should never have married. The court had become an Eastern court, the monarch the muffled centre of sycophants, self-seeking courtiers and harem favourites. It is impossible to see anything in the brief story (2 Sam. 15–19) but weakness in one who had once been strong, and the alienation from the world at large and his people of one who had been once a beloved leader of men.

**2** Perhaps news from beyond his precarious frontiers first alerted David to the peril in which he stood. Like Augustus in a later, wider world, he had set out to stabilize the realm and had put down many enemies. His small empire extended from the borders of Egypt and the Gulf of Aqabah to the upper Euphrates. Fulfilled, secure, deluded by ease, wearied by long toil, the king fell into a species of torpor, illustrated most strikingly by that insensitivity to popular opinion, to personal sin and remoteness of mind from which Nathan, on a notable occasion, bravely awakened him. Events subsequent to Absalom's rebellion revealed how imperilled the frontiers were. As on the occasion of Nathan's rebuke, David, if this conjecture is correct, awoke with a start to life and to reality. It is significant that his first reaction is remembrance of the divine commission of which, in his most perilous days, he never lost awareness. He was anointed by God. It is well to find an anchor in old and genuine experience. David could not forget the day in his youth when Samuel came to Bethlehem, and a commission became his, vindicated in wilderness experience. The 'wilderness' was looming again.

**3** Put the verse in quotation marks. From powerful Damascus round through the villages of Edom and on to the desert raiders of the Negeb, the Amalekites, the word ran in a catchy verse of poetry. 'Now is the hour . . .'

**4** But, thought the menaced man, if God was the establisher of his throne, such rebellion was against the Almighty, against whom strife was absurd. Perhaps a worldly appraisal might call such faith naïve, but it was at this point that the psalm assumed the tinge of prophecy. All sin is part of a larger whole, and when God is opposed in some petty corner of life, the opponent becomes a partner of the hostile host of Calvary. Personal tragedy can mirror the plight of the race – a deep insight of Aristotle, when he saw in tragic drama, a 'purging of the emotions of pity and fear'. When anything is, in utter faith, committed to God, good emerges. Sometimes under such conditions the veils of time grow thin and the shape of wider truth and future happenings appears.

**5** The theme continues. The rhythm becomes thunderous, as though heaven rolled into action.

**Read Psalm 2.6–12; Psalm 110; Acts 4.25–27; Hebrews 1.1–5**

**6** And a voice was heard. Zion was more than an acropolis. It was a holy place, and God had placed a throne there. It was His stronghold. Psa. 110 takes up this hint. Such a king, so appointed, had the touch of one who once had reigned there, another millennium before, the royal priest, Melchizedek.

**7** The speakers in this strange dialogue change. It is David now remembering that, if God was Kingmaker, He was also Father. Psa. 89.26,27 takes up this thought, but in the New Testament a more majestic interpretation emerges (Acts 4.25,26; Heb. 1.5). It is a striking example of God's way with experience committed to Him. The Eternal can universalize the things of Time. 'The man who is following God's will,' runs J. B. Phillips' translation of 1 John 2.17, 'is part of the permanent . . .' So it is with all that is and happens, from loaves and fishes to suffering and joy, when all such are left in Almighty Hands to fashion and transform.

**8** The result of this conversation is a burst of confidence. David was soon to beat his strategic retreat straight towards one of the menaced frontiers, and he needed the courage which flowed into him. This is often the pattern in the psalms. It was once called 'praying through' – continuing, that is, in supplication until, with the adjustments that prayer prompts, and the faith which the very act of prayer engenders, the suppliant bursts into gratitude for the answer. Time contracts. The future answer flows into the present.

**9** There is archaeological evidence for the symbolical smashing of pots inscribed with execration texts. It is perhaps to this custom that the writer refers. The shattered vase is beyond mending, its very clay beyond any reprocessing.

**10,11** It is wisdom, indeed, in ruler and in ruled, to observe, as the appeal bids, the laws of history. There is a moral law woven with the very structure of life which determines the rise and fall of nations, and realization of that fundamental truth may be documented from the Old Testament historians and the Greek Herodotus to Arnold Toynbee.

**12** It is observed that the word for 'son' is the Aramaic *bar*, not the Hebrew *ben* of v. 7. This has caused conjecture since the days of Jerome, and variant readings have been suggested. It has also been maintained for this reason that the verse must have been written after Aramaic became the lingua franca of the Eastern Mediterranean, not a sound assumption, for the rest of the verse is Hebraic enough. Surely, apart from a desire to avoid a discordant rhyming assonance with the next word (*pen*) the reason is that the chief of the restless rebel tribes on the threatened borders was that of the

Aramaeans. Is not a touch of authenticity added by the use of an Aramaic word for the vital noun in the exhortation?

**Conclusion**

A vigorous, passionate psalm ends in a proclamation almost evangelical. David's cry is absorbed naturally into a messianic significance. There can be no greater honour for those who speak out to God to find they speak for God and with God, and utter words in time that echo in Eternity.

# 3

**Read Psalm 3; 2 Samuel 15.1–18; 16.5–14**

**Occasion and author**

Tradition must never be lightly set aside, and ancient rabbinical comment locates this psalm in history. Stung to renewed vigour of mind by the impact of unexpected peril, David had gathered his few faithful followers and commenced the great retreat to the wilderness. It was a political risk to move out towards a potentially hostile eastern frontier. It was a military risk to move out of Jerusalem on the southern side, with Absalom at Hebron, and so to undertake a march with the enemy on the flank. Help, however, lay in that direction. The old guerrilla fighter was withdrawing to the sources of his strength, the sheeplands of the transjordan hills, where the population was with him – an essential in all guerrilla war. They had crossed the Kidron, and made what distance they could before dark. Scouts on the right flank, no doubt, watched the road to Hebron and the refugees camped at night with some relief that no pursuit was visible . . . The king awoke in the sleeping laager with the break of dawn, and the words of the psalm are his morning prayer. They are poignantly true to the heart and mind of man.

**Commentary**

**1,2** The mood of such a moment is familiar enough to those who have known stress and sorrow. Awake with a start from the sleep of deep exhaustion, David knew the sudden inrush of pain. Yesterday, with its taunts, insults, the spectacle of disloyalty, cold fear, the sense of loneliness and isolation . . . The revelation of the strength behind the rebellion had horrified him. Hence the thrice repeated 'many' in the psalm (RSV), reduced to two in the KJV and several other versions: 'God, how *many* are those that oppress me, *many* are in revolt against me, *many* are saying of my soul, No help for him in God.'

The words of Shimei outside the city wall were jangling in his ears. Other voices of like bitter truth had taken shape amid the shouting of the coward mob. He remembered with shame the sin which had undermined his influence, and made him powerless in his own home to rebuke Absalom. And at such moments a beaten man is prone to a dire temptation. Perhaps the crowd spoke truth and there was indeed 'no help for him in God'? He was called to swift review. Just as then, with an old fighting-man's instinct, he was backing on his base, so too must he go back to past forgiveness, and remember what he had done to set evil right with God. Perhaps the words of public penitence, which we call Psa. 51, came with solace to his lips and brought him needed peace. He must hold that fast.

**3** He lay there in the paling dawn, his shield over him to roof him from the dew, and as the words of old repentance wove themselves into the day's first supplication the arched leather of his buckler assumed pictorial significance. The shield was like God, a wall against the stinging shafts which flew at him. He could at last, as men can, if faith be firm, forgive himself for the sins which God Himself had forgiven. Glory, as man counted glory, was in the dust with the royal robes of yesterday. God gave his spirit strength to slip his arm through the shield's straps and 'lift his head'. Sleeping men were stirring round him on the bare hillside. The ridge beyond which the city lay was dark behind him. The sky was opal above the wall of the Moab hills, and it was silent, still, save for a muffled voice here, a clink of metal there. There had been no night attack, thank God.

**4** Prayer, in a word, was answered. A scout, perhaps, came in with news that there was no movement of pursuit all along the line of yesterday's retreat. It had been a night of peril. Cretans and Philistines, men of the same race, had formed part of his bodyguard (2 Sam. 15.18), and the record shows that the men of the coastal plain were prone to panic in a night atack. It was that fault which Jonathan and his brave armour-bearer had once known how to turn to good account. He was safe. The thought deserved a moment's pause and contemplation as, in old habit, David's prayer began to fall into the shape of a song. 'Selah' came a second time.

**5** Yes, he had slept, and that was miracle enough for a heart so burdened. Absalom unaccountably, save that God confused him, had withheld the hand which, in swift attack, might that very night have made his seizure of the kingdom sure. God had 'sustained', for none else had, His embattled anointed.

**6** The prayer was half way through and, as prayer sometimes does, was shaping its own answer. He uses again obliquely the word *rôb* (many), which the first sentences had contained three times. In the light of the new faith and courage flowing through him, the multitude of his foes seemed, to the psalmist, a mere horde, insignificant in God's sight. They were 'round about' in very truth, to the south-west, where the long ridge of the Judean uplands was a sharp edge now against the lightening sky, to the north through the far reaches of the tribal lands where the son of Jesse had never found acceptance, those provinces which, with lapse of time, were to break disastrously away from the south. And across the path, through the descending ridges towards Jordan where the rest of the march stretched, who could know what ambush might be waiting?

**7** Something, however, told the soldier in him that victory was won, and faith took and shaped that confidence into an affirmation. The rebellion had failed at its first testing. It lacked the resolution to attack. The battle for Absalom was lost by that first night's failure to act. Let the old lion but reach his den, and the hunt had lost its quarry. And the lion was a day's march on the way. Hence the confident assertions of this verse of strong triumph. Prayer has broken through.

**8** Just as v. 6 bent back on vs. 1 and 2, v. 8 replies to v. 2. God alone can save. And in such preservation could lie blessing for the land. David had burst through the barrier of his own anxieties. Resentment against a supine host who had not rallied to their king, who, seduced by the handsome, treacherous prince, had turned from the one who had made their borders safe, seems now lost in pity. He can pray for 'God's people', for surely the last words of the psalm encompass a greater number than the little band on the hillside just north of the Jericho road, who were forming line, eating a hasty crust, and buckling on their arms. Light was flooding the blue distances of the Jordan Valley. It seemed a symbol of hope renewed. Pause and think of that – *Selah* – for whatever in the liturgy of the Psalter this word may mean, it never occurs except where some weighty word calls for emphasis, attention or adornment. Forward, men, there is a long day ahead!

**Read Psalm 4; 2 Samuel 16.15–23; 17.1–14**

**Occasion**

A long day it was, with the words of the morning prayer ringing like 'ballad burthen music' in his heart. It is easy to see this happening as the words of the evening prayer (8) took form and shape in the poet's mind over the long dusty miles. Observe the echoes – 'my glory' (2, KJV), 'there are many who say' (6), 'I will both lie down and sleep' (8). The march must have swung north-east away from the long, descending curves of the Jericho road, across the rougher country where remembered tracks led to the Jordan at a point opposite the Jabbok Gorge, the straight road to Mahanaim. There was arduous marching there, but it was no place for cavalry, and ideal guerrilla country. Absalom's procrastination must have seemed incredible to David, but the volatile fool in the prince was enjoying the plaudits of men, and savouring all the looted fruits of royalty. All day long David tramped with his men, looking behind for the distant cloud of dust which might indicate pursuit. The screen of scouts, coming in each hour, had nothing to report. The 'fifth column', back in Jerusalem, was doing good work to promote Absalom's deadly delay.

**Commentary**

**1** David now no longer felt trapped. Hence this verse so clumsily translated in the KJV. George Adam Smith rendered: 'In narrow places you have made space for me'. 'O God, my champion,' wrote Moffatt, '. . . When I was hemmed in, thou hast freed me often.' This fits in with the mood of the second day's retreat. David had abandoned Jerusalem to find space for action. He cast off an urban claustrophobia, which was as spiritual as it was military. He knew from long experience that the desert was friendly. Often, hemmed in by one of Saul's patrols, he had 'run through a troop', as he puts it elsewhere (Psa. 18.29, KJV), and, by some hidden ravine, sheep track or cavern, had escaped. He was seeking such tactical withdrawal on the wider strategic scale, and there is a deep lesson in the act for the denizens of harsh urban environments. When evil closes in, a bold breakthrough to the familiar uplands, scenes of old deliverance, clean air, and freedom, is sound practice.

**2** The second verse, as was remarked above, resumes a thread of the morning's thought. The land at large had turned the king's royal dignity to shame. It is part of the baseness of man to love the degradation of the great, the monarch in the tumbril, the fallen leader . . . Browning put it well in his little poem *The Patriot* – and especially its concluding verse.

*Thus I entered, and thus I go!*
*In triumphs, people have dropped down dead.*
*'Paid by the world, what dost thou owe*
*Me?' – God might question; now instead,*
*'Tis God shall repay: I am safer so.*

David was learning that lesson. God had stripped away the tinsel and in the ageing man in rough combat dress, trudging beside his troops, there was little to suggest the king. And yet he had a royalty greater than he knew. He had called God his glory that morning (3.3), and God's glory suffered in the shame of one whom God had owned. It was the richness of that thought which was to enable the psalmist in the royal soldier to make one more contribution to the literature of man and the Word of God – the Psalms of the Great Rebellion. As for the benighted people, the active betrayers, and the silent majority, those who had loved 'vanity' and made false values their quest, David could only wonder how long their delusion would endure.

**3** The train of thought carries on. Vanity, empty goods, were and are the quest of the majority of mankind. Bunyan lists the merchandise on sale in the market place of Vanity Fair, 'places, honours, titles, lusts, pleasures and delights of all sorts such as whores, bawds, bodies, souls, silver, gold, precious stones . . .' Such fodder does not sustain real life. Dante met, in the vestibule of Hell, a misty multitude chasing a floating banner, the host of those who, in the great day of choosing, had been neither for God nor the Devil. They had never been really alive, not owned of God because they had never sided with Him. Hence the sudden thrilling thought that God sets the godly apart for

Himself. God's remnant, tramping down the paths to Jordan, were 'God's people'. The rest were not significant, numerous though their host might be. 'I would not have believed that death could have undone so many,' gasped Dante in a line which T. S. Eliot significantly lifted to put into *The Waste Land*.

**4** Footsore, watching the further walls of Jordan grow higher as the sun sloped, David felt his mind glow with a new clarity. He could see the reason for it all. Reverence for God is the key to moral living. Awe, 'the fear of the Lord', reverence for all He stands for, is lost only with mortal peril.

At the same time awe, reverence, the fear of God, if you will, is a real and salutary experience, and is lost with spiritual peril. Man diminishes God when he exalts himself, and self-assertion is a prime ingredient of sin, and the rebellion which it indicates. The Greeks were sensitive in this sphere of thought. They explained much history in a sequence of three words: *koris, hubris, atê*. With considerable loss of moral content the words may be translated 'surfeit', 'arrogant behaviour' and 'disaster'. The first suggests the demoralization which comes with prosperity or too complete success, the relaxing of the moral fibre in the favoured of fortune; the second implies the consequent loss of mental and moral balance reflected in over-confidence and outrageous action. Jeshurun, as the Hebrew parable puts it, waxes fat and kicks. The third word, also oddly Hebraic in force, contains the notion of the mad, blind impulse by which the spirit, morally ripe for disaster and in the grip of sin unpardonable, is driven into the catastrophic folly of attempting the impossible.

Perhaps David saw, in the terms of his own thought, the out-working of such a moral law in his own recent story. The ease of royalty, affluence, the city and achievement, had been a poisonous climate for his soul. Perhaps he saw how 'awe', and all he meant of self-abnegation by that word, had decayed. Herodotus, who built his history of the Persian War round the triple sequence, would certainly have seen the arrogant Absalom as a prime illustration of what an insolent scorn of God and good can do to a man.

Sin is holding lightly the things of God. It may be illustrated from all forms of sin. Lust is treating the gift of love with contempt. Lying and sham are handling truth with irreverence. The fool abuses his body, that temple of God's abiding, with contempt. Man at large has used the world, its soil, its air, its water with selfish scorn, and the bill is now presented. Inevitably man reaps what he sows. This verse is the heart of the psalm. David knew that the thought would stay with him when darkness fell, and he spread his cloak on the hard ground to sleep. If these words were already a song, versed and accompanied for the evening hymn of the refugees, some may have done what the psalmist had done all day, faced life afresh with all the loose trappings torn away and with reality exposed. Life sometimes compels such confrontation with helplessness and ruthless truth.

**5,6** And the sacrifices of God, as David had once before said, are 'a broken spirit and a contrite heart' (Psa. 51.17). Such realization is a prerequisite of prayer. The leader of the little band calls his men to bow their hearts and trust, for had not some of them found the day too daunting? Marching with the column, he had caught a note or two of murmuring and complaint. It is the way of the weary soldier to look with a sombre eye on the day's hardships. The limestone hills made tough marching, rations were meagre, and some were wondering whether all would be well. 'Who will show us any good?' they grumbled. 'Who will give us a taste of happiness, some confidence in victory?' 'What are we to get out of this forlorn expedition?' A paralysing thought was that to run along the ranks . . . The sun was going down behind them. The Moab ridges ahead were purple against the darkening sky. Let God be the sunrise on the tired and weary minds of his harassed men, this is the leader's prayer. 'Let your face shine upon us, like a sun which goes not down.'

**7,8** He, in fact, sensed a thrill of jubilation. No attack had come all through that vital day. He felt as he felt when a boy at Bethlehem, and when the corn was in with no disaster of storm to mar the welcome harvest. There was no sign that any pursuit was on the way. He could sleep now, safe in God's hollowed hand. God had, he felt deeply sure, made him safe. The stars came out. He was weary to the bone. His song was sung. Some at least had the words thrumming in their minds. He knew that sleep would fall upon him, the cares of last night quenched.

**Conclusion**

The moods of a perilous twelve hours, dawn to dark, have made moving reading. We have allowed imagination to play around the two psalms, imagination triggered by the rabbinical hint at the head of Psa. 3, and led on by the brief record in the second book of Samuel, along with a study of the map of the retreat. Pain, defeat, retreat, rejection – all these, like all that which might be counted evil, can be turned to fruit and usefulness, if they can but be committed to God's creative hands. Picture the dust and the sweat, feel the heat of the day, and hear the tread of marching men behind the words of these two songs, and those words assume vividness, and the train of thought becomes clear. From trough to peak the mood has passed in sixteen verses. The trough is to be known again, as is also the high peak, but that is the way with man. It should be ever remembered that God's Spirit is no seabird flicking the wave-tops only. He rides the waters, down between the waves and on their dizzy, curling peaks.

# 5

**Read Psalm 5; Hebrews 10.19–22**

**Occasion and author**

The suggestion in v. 3 that this is a morning prayer, and the echo of the image of the shield in v. 12, make it likely that the editor of the psalms rightly placed this song in the sequence of pieces which took shape during the retreat to Jordan. The same thoughts haunt the psalm, the cry for guidance in a day which needed wisdom, with hostility and treachery abroad, are further argument to this end. Another night has passed. The march had ended at the foot of the great Rift Valley where the twisting Jordan meanders through a jungle-ridden plain. River and plain were no great military obstacle except to chariots and cavalry, difficult though the terrain was for a weary band of tired men to struggle through, but David may have had news of the rejection of Ahithophel's plan of swift and hard pursuit, and felt within reach of safety. It was wild country just ahead, but beyond, lay friends and rest and safety. No doubt reconnaissance up and down the stream confirmed the emptiness of the land, but it was a day's hard struggle which lay ahead, and prayer was needed. From the low slopes they could see only wilderness.

Nelson Glueck writes: 'The narrow flood plain of the Zor, through which the Jordan knifes its way, is tropical in character, and for the most part, lush green in colour. Its vegetation is rank, and thorn and thistle grow shoulder-high. It is covered with dense and at times almost impenetrable thickets of oleander, cane, tangled bushes, vines, willows, poplars and twisted tamarisks.'

Sir George Adam Smith, in his great book on the geography of Palestine, writes vividly of the Zor: 'In many parts are mounds and ridges of grey marl, salt and greasy, with stretches of gravel, sand, clay and other debris of an old sea-bottom, that assume the weirdest shapes, and give a desolate aspect to the Vale. But notwithstanding this poison, vegetation is rank, especially in spring. The heat is of a forcing-house. Wherever water comes, the flowers rise to the knee, and herbage often to the shoulder. The drier stretches are covered by broom or intricate thorn-bush. By all the streams there are brakes of cane and oleander. The streams dash down to the Jordan, tearing up the surface of the country by their spring floods, and heaping across flowers and grass the loosened marl and ruin of cane-brake. Swamps abound and there is much malaria . . . To those who look down from the hills along any great stretch of the Valley, this Zor, as it is called, trails and winds like an enormous green serpent, more forbidding in its rankness than any open water could be . . .'

This was the 'luxuriance' or 'rankness' of Jordan, called the 'pride' or 'swelling' of Jordan in the KJV, a haunt and covert of wild beasts, a truly formidable barrier on the route to safety, if a sure defence against immediate pursuit, and eventual attack. The leader looked down on such a scene from some point on the western high country which cannot be certainly identified.

It is possible to mark on a map the line of march if it can be assumed that the Jabbok Gorge is the vestibule of the uplands round Mahanaim which was David's haven and goal. From the refugees' point of view, the path would lead away from the first leg out of Jerusalem, where Hebron and dire danger menaced an exposed flank. The first pursuit might naturally, if it materialized, drive down the ancient trail to the Jordan fords near Jericho, roughly on the line of the present road. A swerve north-north-east might be difficult to conceal, but the king was an old guerrilla fighter, and might know how to confuse the enemy by sending some of his heavier elements treading the road to Jericho with orders to cut north and join the main group on the hills to the left of the road, where concealment might be quite simple.

**Commentary**

**1,2** Prayer is envisaged as words, meditation, a cry. 'Listen to my words,' Moffatt's version runs, 'and hear the murmur of my soul . . . give ear to my appeal.' Prayer can be ordered utterance, the petition 'directed' (3) to God in coherent speech. It can also be the uplifted longing of the heart which can find no specific words but which God Himself can understand and phrase – 'sighs too deep for words' (Rom. 8.26) as the RSV puts it, or 'agonising longings which never find words' in J. B. Phillips' rendering. The 'cry' of v. 2 is the ejaculation of distress, the appeal for help in emergency or crisis of the man habitually given to reaching out for aid. As David looked over the tangled plain towards the crease in the jungle green where the river ran, he could only cry for aid. And there was no one else to whom he could appeal.

**3** 'I set forth my plea, waiting thine answer,' says Moffatt. A thoughtful prayer together with an expectant faith is in the words. David is framing a prayer for his men, and a responsibility not always recognized lies on those who presume to gather up the desires and longings of others, to give them clarity and comprehensiveness and to present them to God. There is no reason why such a prayer should not be prepared as a sermon is prepared. Those who lead in public prayer have no right to confine utterance to self-expression, to make their words a demonstration of rhetoric or an exhibition of theological knowledge. They give words and form to others' thoughts and should recognize the need to order and 'set forth' their plea. The verse ends with confidence that the King (2) addressed will hear. David has his own hall of audience in mind. For a subject to appear there was a matter of moment. It was a privilege which called for gratitude, proper circumspection, words appropriate to the high occasion.

**4** Hence the need for preparation. To approach the shrine of Apollo where the temple of the oracle stands on the ledge above the awesome Peneus Gorge at Delphi, the suppliant first washed in the Castalian Spring. The water pours out, clean from the snows of Parnassus, at the foot of the Phaidriades – the Shining Cliffs. The Sacred Way, deliberately flexed and long, led the procession up to the columned temple, with its statutary adornment and the uplifted command: 'Know thyself'. The mighty landscape solemnized the soul; the great gorge below, the coloured precipices above, the blue distances towards the Corinth gulf beyond the olive green of the Amphissian plain.

It was the same in Athens. As the annual procession wound up to Athena's shrine, the wondrous Parthenon, the moment of confrontation with the great mellow temple was postponed until a precise moment. The worshippers had come up the long winding slope through the Propylaea, and suddenly, with a sense of awe which even the modern visitor can sense, the vision of beauty broke on the sight . . . The deep instinct of the old pagan cults, at Delphi, at Athens – and at Eleusis with its crisis moment of the uplifted ear of corn, was to make those who approached the deity aware of a majesty to be confronted, a privilege to be prized and held with reverent hands. To be sure, as the writer to the Hebrews puts it, Christ has broken down the veil which screened the Holy Place, and opened up a 'new and living way', but it should still be an occasion of reverence, and no act of squalid haste to penetrate into the presence of the King. Hence the musing of four verses, for God, the psalmist says, has no pleasure in wickedness, and will house no evil in His dwelling-place. If His dwelling-place be the human personality, it is well to initiate prayer with self-examination.

**5,6** In this act of self-awareness David thinks of folly (5, KJV), falsehood and harm done to a fellow man. They were sins which he himself had known, and of which he had bitterly repented. Folly is an ingredient of all sin – the very basis of some sin. In one of the most solemn parables of Christ, God calls a man who mistook his body for his soul, and who thought the future a matter which he could control, a fool. Falsehood is another deep corruption. 'Sin,' said Oliver Wendell Holmes, 'has many tools, but a lie is the handle that fits them all.' David knew that he could illustrate that truth from the story of his own sin and Bathsheba's.

**7** 'Bold I approach the eternal throne,' runs Wesley's hymn. 'I then encompassed by thy mercy,' runs Ronald Knox's rendering of this verse, 'will betake myself to thy house, and in reverence of thee bow down before thy sanctuary.' The ridge beyond which Jerusalem lay was out of sight. The Ark of the Covenant remained there behind its curtains, a symbol of David's faith that he would return. When he and his men prayed their morning prayer, they perhaps turned and faced south-west towards the abandoned city, their foes and the symbol of God's presence with His people.

Such musing and preparation of soul could well have been the groaning (RSV) or 'meditation' (KJV) of the opening movement of the psalm. Words of specific meaning were used, for the prayer was for public use, but behind those words lay the unuttered confessions of personal wrongdoing, and the remembered pattern of sin which God alone and the sinner knew. If we may thus divide the psalm on the hint of its first three verses, the cry, the plea or the appeal, as it is variously rendered, now follows, as the psalmist asks for special aid.

**8** Two prayers are in this verse. 'Let not any foes triumph over me, for

Thou art righteous'; and 'make my path straight before my face' . . . To stand and look east was to see first the rough terrain of the valley floor, then the dark and rocky path beyond the river up the forbidding canyon of the Jabbok. And to lift the eyes beyond the horizon and look in imagination further east was itself to court a twinge of doubt. Beyond the chosen base of Mahanaim and what David trusted would be friendly territory, were the vassal border states in restless subjection. In faith David proposed to march straight through the physical obstacles at his feet and on towards what might be hostile confrontation. Life often calls for such resolution. Like a Roman road, God's path, never other than a way of righteousness, cuts straight through towards its goal.

**9,10** Like the 'cries' of v. 2, these words seem like a sudden outburst. Some wave of resentment, even in the midst of ordered prayer, has overwhelmed the mind, and David, as his custom was, pours it out before God. It is better thus. If the heart is hot it is good to give it words where the words can find their answer and the heat can find assuagement.

**11,12** The healing is obvious and the mood quietens as the psalm ends. The rebels raved far over the hills, but the rebels were already doomed. God's shield was high above the little company, and if for a brief hot moment David had looked too closely at the foe, his head was lifted now. Fénélon once said: 'Peace does not dwell in outward things but in the soul. We may preserve it in the midst of the bitterest pain, if our will remain firm and submissive. Peace in this life springs from acquiescence, not in exemption from suffering.' If David had never grasped that lesson before, he grasped it with both hands that morning just above the last slope which fell away to the green jungle round the twisting river. Fénélon touched Isaiah's theme: 'Thou wilt keep him in perfect peace whose mind is stayed on thee' (26.3). Knox here achieves a rendering which does justice to the repetition of the word 'peace' in the Hebrew: 'Our thoughts wayward no longer, thou wilt maintain us in peace, peace that comes surely to those who trust in thee. Yours to trust in the Lord continually, the Lord that is evermore your protection.'

The psalm ends with peace achieved. It shows the fortifying of the soul, and the calming of the mind which are the first fruits of prayer . . . The march resumed, single column now, and slow, through the rough scrub-oak and the tumbled stony valley bottom.

**Read Psalm 6; John 12.20–28**

**Occasion and author**

There is again no valid reason to question the traditional authorship. The psalm also maintains the alternation of day and night (6). Night seems to be far spent, and a guess may be hazarded about where it was spent. The column had battled through the Jordan jungle. They had crossed the river. They would pause, in utter exhaustion, at the point where the Jabbok Gorge came down to the plain. Up that ravine, and twenty-five miles away, lay the rallying place of the king's men. Everything would suggest a further march in spite of the advancing afternoon. The Jordan was behind and danger from the rear was now minimal. Anxiety about what might lie ahead, with a doubtful frontier beyond Mahanaim, might correspondingly sharpen. David would remember Jacob and his grim night conflict by that same tributary of Jordan. It was an oppressive landscape with the high hills closing in on the valley track as evening fell. Sleep came hard on this third night. Bodily exhaustion was eroding the spirit's resources, and the lively imagination of the poet was making phantoms out of the darkness. It is well to remember in the darkness that which God has clearly shown us in the light, but it is not always easy to lay hold of such victory.

**Commentary**

**1,2** These words are the cry of a desperately weary man. Doubt haunts the night. The dark cliffs, the narrow ribbon of starlight above, the noise of the stream, all spoke of abandonment and prompted the sick thought of God's displeasure. The sun is down in more ways than one, and David cries for help. God never mistakes the voice of pain for the voice of impiety. The God who would have us weep with those who weep is not a God to frown upon anxiety, depression and agony of mind. Nothing rings more harshly and cruelly than the calm rebukes which insulated piety or constitutional euphoria is accustomed to administer, homiletically divided, to victims of melancholy and stress. Holding, as David was at this moment, to a tattered faith, desperate for comfort and strength, such afflicted folk need no precepts on the 'sin of anxiety'. They need encouragement to pray and to tell God everything.

**3,4** David does. He knew that his soul reflected the body's utter weariness and though God seemed, in the long night watch, to tarry, He yet would 'turn', 'deliver', 'save'. The Lord actually quoted part of v. 3 (John 12.27).

The phrase 'for the sake of thy steadfast love' reveals the whole cast of the suppliant's thought. He was holding fast to the memory of 'love in time past', which, as John Newton put it,

*Forbids me to think*
*He'll leave me at last*
*In trouble to sink.*

**5** Confidence in another life was a gift of the New Testament, and a resurrected Christ. At the same time, there is more concerning such a faith in the Old Testament than some are prepared to concede. Merely to move on to Psa. 16, and look at the last four verses, is indication of this. There is also no reason to regard Psa. 16 as late and not Davidic. The closing verse of Psa. 17 suggests the same lively hope. Pss. 49.15 and 73.24 imply a similar faith. The last-named psalm, in fact, seems to reach out to Paul's triumphant passage at the end of Rom. 8.

The sombre words in v. 5 must be read in the light of the whole dark context of this prayer. The words are an utterance of near-despair, and it is part of the value of psalms like this that they reveal, along with the anguish of the human soul, something of the love and understanding which meet the need. There is health in frankness. The psalmist's faith has worn thin. He follows one remaining instinct, and that suffices. He still holds to God, though hope has narrowed, the horizon closed and the path grown dark.

**6,7** When the soul is thus burdened it is best to put it into words and set it before God. This psalm was probably a private prayer, not one intended for the company. It is David speaking intimately to God, and those who have known the weary weight of an almost intolerable anxiety will understand this voice of complaining. It is a fair guess that none of his men knew what racked the leader's mind as the sky grew faintly pale above the canyon walls and the night passed.

**8–10** The mood, in fact, dramatically changes. As though springing to his feet to repel a night attack with reinforcements pouring in to aid, David bids iniquity depart. His cry is heard and the foe scatters. Cowper, who knew, in like fashion, the dark night of the soul, was also conscious of such moments.

*Sometimes a light surprises*
*The Christian while he sings:*
*It is the Lord who rises*
*With healing in His wings;*
*When comforts are declining,*
*He grants the soul again*
*A season of clear shining,*
*To cheer it after rain.*

With morning brightening and the light penetrating what had been a valley of the shadow of death, David realized that the retreat was over. Mahanaim was a half-day's march ahead. Victory was won. Psa. 23 was to be his next poem if the sequence of psalm and history is read aright. Psa. 23 might, in fact, have been placed next in order.

# 7

**Read Psalm 7; 1 Samuel 24**

**Occasion and author**

There is no reason to doubt the Davidic authorship of this passionate psalm. To locate the occasion in the surviving record is more difficult. Was Cush, of the tribe of Benjamin, Shimei, whose abusive words pursued David out of Jerusalem? Or was he rather an unknown slanderer of earlier days – one, perhaps, of those to whom David refers in the dramatic story of 1 Sam. 24? It is impossible to say, but his slander, as slander and lies always did, stirred the psalmist to fierce protest. Hence this *shiggaion*. The word baffles translation. Moffatt, picking up a Greek word from the worship of Dionysus and the complicated style of hymn associated with it, translates 'dithyramb'. To a classicist the word will sound a trifle odd. 'The meaning', writes Ian Maclaren in his perceptive commentary, 'is unknown, and commentators who do not like to say so, have much ado to find a meaning.' The root is a verb meaning 'to wander', and the explanation is sometimes given that the word describes the disconnected utterance of the psalm, a collection of succeeding emotions rather than of sequent thoughts. It is difficult to imagine that a name would be given to such a style of writing. It is not, after all, an unnatural style in storm-tossed prayer, and David is in a wild mood of protestation and ejaculatory petition. He is not 'ordering a prayer' as in Psa. 5, nor so sombrely defeated as in Psa. 6. The tone is high and courageous, challenging and sure, and not so disconnected as at first reading appears.

**Commentary**

**1,2** A cry for help goes well with a protestation of faith. David looks to his God before looking at the perils that pursue him, and chief of those perils were those out to rend his 'soul' (KJV), and all that word contains, as a lion might tear a man's body. The lion was a common enough peril of the Judean wilderness. The royal beast survived in Palestine until the Crusades, in Syria until the last century, a symbol of strength, swift pursuit, deadly assault. Cush was such a beast, and the attack was a bitter and effective one.
**3–5** And this, he protests, might be due judgement, had it been in fair recompense for wrong done, for injustice practised, or for persecution. But it was not. It was jealousy, that 'fume of little minds', which prompted the malice. It is a dark fact that men hate goodness itself when its clean presence reveals their own darkness. Aristides was called 'the Just' in fifth-century

Athens, and one day, when the city was voting on his exile, Aristides found an ignorant peasant seeking someone to write his name on the voting ticket. He obliged and asked the fellow why he wished to exile Aristides. 'Because,' said the boor, 'I'm sick of hearing him called the Just.' Some of those scraps of pottery bearing Aristides' name survive, small monuments to human vice.

**6,7** Aristotle, the great Greek thinker, once made a perceptive remark on the function of tragic drama. It 'purged the emotions of pity and of fear'. He seemed to say that the great plays had a cleansing function. The fate of tragic heroes and heroines universalized emotion, and made men see that, in their own sufferings and pain, they were part of a whole, a sharer in mankind. Something of this sort happens to the prayer, and gives a sequence and coherence which might otherwise elude. David sees his agony of mind in the light of mankind's problem of universal sin and injustice. Sin against any man is a sin against the Lord . . . 'Father, I have sinned against heaven and in thy sight . . .' The final remedy could only be in God's judgement on universal sin. Wrong done to Him was wrong done to humanity, and wrong done to any man was iniquity before the Lord.

**8,9** And slander itself, the widening concept realizes, can only be part of more comprehensive sin. Good men long for the ultimate solution. The weary years seem to bring no relief, no intervention from on high. And yet, except earth be darkness to the core, there must be One who cares. We, at the other end of history, see the demonstration, and know that God marks and waits, for He did in truth, once for all, decisively, intervene. As James Russell Lowell put it:

> *Careless seems the great Avenger; history's pages but record*
> *One death-grapple in the darkness 'twixt old systems and the Word:*
> *Truth forever on the scaffold, Wrong forever on the throne, –*
> *Yet that scaffold sways the future, and, behind the dim unknown,*
> *Standeth God within the shadow, keeping watch above His own.*

**10–13** This is the psalmist's faith. Justice was a Hebrew preoccupation. 'Justice, justice shalt thou pursue', ran the old command (Deut. 16.20), and such passion for fair dealing was founded on the deep faith that God was just. For justice the Old Testament never ceases to plead, and no Hebrew could think of his God as ever less than ultimately just.

**14–17** And then comes a flash of insight. Divine justice worked through a moral law. Just as in the New Testament faith and grace interweave to build salvation, just as man 'works out his own salvation' and by grace, mediated through living, active faith, 'becomes transformed by the renewing of his mind', so evil digs its own pit (15), and organizes its own destruction. Sin is suicidal. It is like a stone thrown up which gravity's inexorable law brings accelerating down upon the thrower's head (16).

**Conclusion**

Observe then the maturity of the whole, and the developing thought from faith (1) to praise (17) through this loud call for aid. The victim of human malice might remember: (i) Justice will prevail (8,9). (ii) Therefore commit it all to God (10). (iii) Evil will prove to contain its own punishment (13–16) . . . And we may remember that the Lord was slandered.

**Read Psalm 8; Acts 17.21–31**

**Occasion and author**

This 'nature psalm', one of five which might thus be named (19,29,65,104 are the others), is traditionally a lyric of David. It could come from any period in his early life. Men in that ancient world were more conscious of the stars than they are today. The constellations hung low and clear, and seemed tremendously significant. Perhaps these are thoughts from the days of youthful shepherding, or from the nights in the silent desert when David fled from Saul.

**Commentary**

**1** The sight of the stars stirred worship. This was Isaiah's point. Many centuries passed over the grave of the shepherd-king before the moving fortieth chapter of Isaiah was written. That great piece of prose-poetry begins with the words of solemn comfort which found their way into Handel's most majestic music. Its theme passes from God's love for His sorely tried people to scorn and satire against idolatry. It closes with a call to look up and consider the might and wonder of celestial creation. 'Lift up your eyes on high,' cried the preacher, 'and see: who created these? He who brings out their host by number, calling them all by name; by the greatness of his might, and because he is strong in power not one is missing' (26).

Sir George Adam Smith, the great geographer of Palestine, and greatest of commentators on Isaiah, points out that this chapter was written for the comfort of exiles in Babylonia. The clock of history was about to strike a new hour. The dominance of cruel Babylon, which had packed the featureless river plain with uprooted exiles from many lands, was about to end. The foresight of the prophet marked the significance of the hour, and indeed, when Persia brought great Babylon down, twenty-five centuries ago, Babylon's victims found their nationhood, if not their freedom, in the act.

But there, says the commentator, amid the confused settlements of those whom the megalomania of Babylon had packed into the vast monotony of the endless river plain, 'there was no escape for the heart but to the stars.' Consider that wide land in Nebuchadnezzar's day. In it were countless families of men torn from their far homes, and crowded promiscuously, with embittered hearts. In that huge servitude ancient liberties were crushed, patriotisms sighed themselves to death amid the tyrant's mud and mortar, histories lay broken and interrupted . . .

'Starry heavens,' men might groan in the tropic night, 'is there a God behind you, who allows one tyrant to crush men in the vat of his power, as they crushed the murex shellfish to provide imperial purple for the royal robes?' In that medley of peoples was Israel, equally lost with the most barbaric tribe, her history severed, her worship made impossible, a despairing breed who remembered only with pain the psalms of her ancient king.

But on the flat plain one could look up. The stars were visible, and on them the preacher bids the desperate survivors fix their gaze. They were a vision of power, order and unfailing precision. 'By the greatness of His might . . . not one is missing.' He continues: 'Why do you say . . ., "My way is hid from the Lord, and my right is disregarded by my God"?' The psalm into which the chapter merges rises in strength and confidence and concludes: 'They who wait for the Lord shall renew their strength, they shall mount up with wings like eagles, they shall run and not be weary, they shall walk and not faint.'

Just as visible as the countless stars in the dark heavens to the eyes of slaves looking up, so were their lives to His eyes which looked down on the tangle of peoples. Let them therefore trust in the ultimate victory of the good, and the final triumph of their God.

**2** Matthew 21.16 seems to be the key. Even the trust of a child is a bulwark against the evil of corrupt men. Extend Christ's words and observe a wider significance. What mood do the constellations stir? How measure values in God's eyes? Lucretius, Rome's Epicurean poet, writing in the atheism of his philosophy, spoke sombrely of the *signa severa*, the 'austere constellations'. George Sand echoed him nineteen centuries later: '. . . the cold stare of the stars which seem to say to us, You are nought but vanity, grains of sand. Tomorrow you will not be, and we shall not know.' In the last word lies the answer, and it is parallel with this verse. One child looking up with awe and wonder at the wheeling stars is a greater marvel than a dead galaxy.

**3,4** The first overwhelming thought at the spectacle of the heavens and their utter mystery is man's insignificance. The steady light of any night sky is only a vision of what was. The viewer looks into immeasurable past time, as well as into immeasurable space, for the light which touches the eye, at any given moment, is light emitted in the distant past – sometimes before human history began. It daunts the mind and stirs the crushing thought of human frailty. But again, is not the mind which can phrase such thought a far greater wonder than the interweaving light which stirs such poetry? Admiral Byrd, alone in Antarctica, spoke of his impression in the lonely months of polar night of 'the inexhaustible evidence of a vast pervading intelligence', and does not the questing, wondering mind which seeks to understand the heavens, reflect that Intelligence in the image in which it was made?

And is not the inexorable face of the heavens which George Sand found so cold and repellent lost in the knowledge that God cares and cherishes the tiny, living, understanding fragment of the whole creation called 'man' and the 'son of man'?

A fundamental question is asked and answered. A considerable anthology could be written on the theme. 'Wonders are many,' writes Sophocles four centuries later than the psalmist, 'and none is more wonderful than man.' 'Man is a political animal,' said Aristotle briskly a century later still. 'Man is a religious animal,' said Edmund Burke. 'Man is a tool-making animal,' answers Benjamin Franklin. 'A tool-using animal,' replies Carlyle. 'Man is heaven's masterpiece,' Francis Quarles had written, long before Burke, Franklin and Carlyle were born. And Gilbert answers, doubtless with Sullivan's approval, 'man is Nature's sole mistake.' 'He is but a devil weakly fettered by some generous beliefs,' said Robert Louis Stevenson. Perhaps Pascal was right: 'Man is only a reed, the weakest thing in Nature, but he is a thinking reed.' This 'embodied paradox', this 'bundle of contradiction', this 'corpse', this 'noble animal', this 'ape', this 'angel', can think. He can ponder the question of his destiny. And in this act, whether it end in joy or melancholy, in discovery or in frustration, man sets himself for ever apart from animal creation.

Above all man is the object of God's love, and that, even more than the God-given quality of self-awareness, thought and moral responsibility, sets man apart from all creation.

**Read Psalm 8.5–9; Genesis 1**

**5** The verse is correctly translated: 'Thou hast made him a little less than God.' It was the Greek Septuagint version which introduced the word 'angels'. It is a legitimate translation, for *elohim* can be used of created beings (Pss. 29.1; 82.1,6). And the Epistle to the Hebrews (2.6–9) perpetuates it. It is characteristic of the writer of that letter that he bases his massive quotation on the version familiar to the Jews of the Hellenistic world and their host of adherents. The statement is not presumptuous. It refers to the creation of man 'in the image of God' (Gen. 1.26).

What is meant by this phrase? In a sentence it means that man's distinctive being, the theme of this verse, consists in knowing himself to be God's creation, known of God and knowing Him, and involved in a summons to listen, to understand and believe. Man bears the rational image of God. If 'in the beginning was an Intelligence which expressed itself', as John's first verse may be rendered, man demonstrates a kinship. The first condition of success in all scientific investigation must be a similarity of intelligence in the investigator, and in the mind which constructed that which he investigates. To read a book we must understand the language in which it is written. More fundamentally still, our minds must be capable of forming the same conceptions as those conceived and expressed by the author. Man finds in himself the same sort of reason which expresses itself in the universe, or he would be unable to understand the universe. 'It seems impossible,' writes the Platonist, A. E. Taylor, 'to give any account of nature which will be true to the facts, without recognizing the presence of a power which works in the very way in which intelligence works in ourselves.' The human reason at work, as the ontological argument has it, is a demonstration of God. And that truth is hidden in the figure of 'God's image in man'.

God's moral image is similarly recognizable. Reason leads man not only to principles of knowledge but also to laws of conduct. He also possesses the power of self-decision. It is this which most clearly constitutes man a person.

Alone in creation he is faced constantly with the call to moral decision. It is a condition born of his responsibility. No one can deprive him of his power of deciding for himself. The only Power which could force him to say 'yes' will not do so because the act of compulsion would alter the constitution of man, and deny the fundamental principle of his creation. Man is free. The power to decide has been conferred upon him, and that power is continually stirred and renewed by God's call. 'Inescapable,' says Brunner, 'far more than the air we breathe, is the law that man must decide, as long as he lives, and at every moment of his life. If man could escape that necessity he would forthwith cease to be human.'

Again, a faint shadow of God's infinitude haunts man. Man is not omnipresent, but he wages tireless war with his physical limitations, girdles the earth, and probes the depths of space. He is not omniscient, but his thirst for knowledge is insatiable. He is not omnipotent, but he seeks power with passion, and in the search has unlocked nature's deepest secrets. It is significant, too, that man cannot escape from the idea of God's perfection. Plato first noticed the fact and expressed it in immortal fantasies, but long before Plato wrote Job had cried for God. The quest haunts all history. Art is its expression. The bird's nest does not pass the limits of the useful. Neither does the beaver's dam nor the spider's web. Man ever thrusts beyond, seeking the transcendent, as though conscious of an urge to assert a higher destiny, and prove himself nature's lord. He acts like one lost or in exile, nostalgic for his home.

**6–8** It is for this reason that man was given his dominion. It was no tyranny and was laden with responsibility. The statement in Gen. 2.15 runs literally: 'God put man in the Garden of Eden to *serve* and to keep it.' None of the thirty or more English versions of this passage risks the simple, meaningful translation. It means precisely what it says. Man keeps the earth by serving it. Instead he has dominated and enslaved it, and the gift has withered in his selfish hands.

Man must learn to reverence nature. He is only part of it. There is a park north of Sydney called the Kuringai Chase, after the tribe who once hunted and fished there, and worked out, as primitive man can, a perfect balance with environment. Native forest clings to the mighty rocks and valleys which give Australia its look of primitive strength. In a chalet devoted to illustration and instruction there are words which I copied on the folder which tell of the objects of the conservationist authorities. Here they are: 'Fire destroys the damp leaf litter which harbours the worms and crustaceans which feed the lyre birds . . . Industrial pollutants draining into park streams kill plants and planktons which feed fish and crustaceans which feed man and bird . . . Natural environment is the product of all time – dollars cannot make it or repair it . . . No plant or animal lives alone. Where there is one there is another upon which it depends for food, support, protection. In a desert, in a swamp, on a plain, or on a mountainside, there are communities of plants and animals of various species. For better or for worse the life of each is related to the others. All living things, both plant and animal, that make up a community depend upon one another and keep their numbers in balance.'

The Bible is warning enough. Look at Isa. 24 (NEB) and think of man-made deserts, dead species, oil-ridden waters, choking smog, dying forests . . .

> *'The earth dries up and withers,*
> *the whole world withers and grows sick;*
> *the earth's high places sicken*
> *and earth itself is desecrated by the feet of those who live in it,*
> *because they have broken the laws, disobeyed the statutes and violated*
> *the eternal covenant.*
> *For this a curse has devoured the earth*
> *and its inhabitants stand aghast.*
> *For this those who inhabit the earth dwindle . . .'*

> 'The third angel blew his trumpet; and a great star shot from the sky, . . . and it fell on a third of the rivers and springs. The name of the star was Wormwood; and a third of the water turned to wormwood, and men in great numbers died of the water because it had been poisoned' (Rev. 8.10f., NEB).

The whole creation, says Paul to the Roman Christians, 'groans and travails' waiting for a new race of men. Chesterton was more than right in his key verse to *The Ballad of the White Horse*: 'Because it is only Christian men guard even heathen things . . .'

**9** The theme resumes. The 'name', in ancient metaphor, contained the essentials of the person: 'How glorious in all creation is the knowledge and the sense of what you are.'

**Conclusion**

Why did the editor and aranger of the Psalter place Psa. 8 precisely here? The next psalm might be placed at Mahanaim, a musing on the weeks of retreat and exile. Did the editor think to place a word of poetic relief after Psa. 6, a night of death's shadow, if the guess has substance that it preserves the mood of darkness in the Jabbok ravine? We can but speculate, but this small gem of poetry is a precious one, even in these days of dimmer, smeared constellations, when man-made points of light thread their fields of calm.

# 9

**Read Psalm 9**

## Occasion and author

There is again no reason, both with this psalm, and the next which is associated with it, to question the traditional Davidic authorship. The occasion is some day of victory and David had known his times of triumph. The editor of the psalms placed it here, perhaps, because he associated its writing with the sombre victory over Absalom's rebel army. If we are correct in ascribing the earlier sequence of poems, Pss. 2–7, to the retreat to Mahanaim, it might be reasonable to follow the story through the gathering of the loyalists' strength and their riposte. Echoes of word and thought also played a part in the editor's choice. The idea of what Aristotle called *peripeteia,* that reversal of fortune, and the return of evil on the head of its perpetrator, appeared at the end of Psa. 7 (14–16). It is repeated in Psa. 9 (15,16). Small details of verbal repetition of this sort seem sometimes to provide a link between psalm and psalm, as we saw in the case of Pss. 3 and 4. Order could be sometimes thus dictated.

## Commentary

**1–6** Victory is within grasp if not accomplished. God has only to be present and evil withers (3), a remark full of truth and insight which may be observed in any man's personal experience. Man loses any battle he chooses to fight on any ground not of God's choosing.

Ultimately, the psalmist reflects, observing the war-ridden lands of his day, institutions of evil perish. 'The towns which thou hast torn up lie in lasting ruin' (6, Moffatt). The prophet Isaiah had this verse in mind when he pictured Babylon, the terror of the nations, as it was one day to be. Set side by side his vivid prophecy with the words of Layard who first wrote of the great city's present desolation in 1853. Isaiah wrote (13.19–22; 14.23, RV):

'Babylon, the glory of kingdoms, the beauty of the Chaldeans' pride, shall be as when God overthrew Sodom and Gomorrah. It shall never be inhabited, neither shall it be dwelt in from generation to generation: neither shall the Arabian pitch tent there; neither shall shepherds make their flocks to lie down there. But wild beasts of the desert shall lie there; and their houses shall be full of doleful creatures; and ostriches shall dwell there, and satyrs shall dance there. And wolves shall cry in their castles, and jackals in the pleasant places . . . I will also make it a possession for the porcupine, and pools of water: and I will sweep it with the besom of destruction, saith the Lord of Hosts.'

And Layard:

'To the vast mound of Babel succeed long, undulating heaps of earth, bricks and pottery. Other shapeless heaps of rubbish cover for many an acre the face of the land. On all sides, fragments of glass, marble, pottery and inscribed brick are mingled with that peculiar nitrous and blanched soil, which, bred from the remains of ancient habitations, checks or destroys vegetation, and renders the site of Babylon a naked and hideous waste. Owls start from the scanty thickets, and the foul jackal skulks through the furrows' (*Nineveh and Babylon*).

**7–10** The theme rises in fine poetry to the climax of vs. 9 and 10. The Hebrew word for 'refuge' or 'stronghold' means a 'secure height', an acropolis, some uplifted crag of rock like those round which many ancient cities grew, Jerusalem, Athens, Rome, Sardis, Pergamum, to name but a few. Troy, whose piled levels crown the escarpment by the Dardanelles, is the most famed in story. To such retreats the peasantry of the countryside withdraw when the foe floods the plain. God is 'a lofty stronghold in desperate hours', and, if the theme may continue into v. 10 in Moffatt's rendering, 'those who know what thou art can trust in thee.' Observe that the metaphor of the 'name' is picked up from Psa. 8.9 – another of the verbal links between adjacent psalms.

**11–14** Perhaps the word picture of God as the 'lofty stronghold' of those who know Him reminds the psalmist of Zion, Jerusalem's 'high place'. He mentions it twice in four verses. God is the Avenger (12), the Redeemer (13), the Saviour (14) to be praised when strife is past, and the city refuge stands open, at 'the gates'. As the stories of Lot and Job show, the gate was the place of trade, fellowship, justice, traffic – it was there that life flowed by, and those who sought to be in the stream of life sat there to see and to be seen. The ruins of more than one Palestinian *tell* show the dual function of the gate. Walls overlap to make a hostile approach hazardous and slow. The portals are enfiladed from protective tower and battlement. But inside there are cool courts and seats where, the battle done, and the enemy withdrawn, the peaceful citizenry can sit. David seeks a testimony and looks on to the time when, all enemies sunk to rest, he can boast of God.

**15–17** Evil contains an element of self-destruction. God's mills grind slowly but in the end a moral law works to an inexorable conclusion. A. J. Toynbee's monumental work on history demonstrated from a score of human cultures, which have left clear record of their rise and fall, that all human progress is built round a core of moral ideas and ideals which give it character and strength. When that core, that ethos, decays, the culture itself, after a brief time-lag, follows. There is an inbuilt certainty of retribution for group and individual, and he is deceived who imagines the brief delay a guarantee of immunity.

**18** The 'needy', the victims of evil, the oppressed, the sufferers of wrong, 'shall not always be forgotten' nor 'the hope of the poor perish for ever.' 'The poor', or as Moffatt puts it, 'the downtrodden' are a theme of Isaiah, mentioned in a passage quoted by the Lord in the synagogue at Capernaum, and the subject of the first of the Beatitudes. The thought again rises that Isaiah had this psalm frequently in mind. We have referred to his thirteenth chapter. Look, also, at ch. 25, especially vs. 4 and 8, and follow it through to ch. 61 and back to ch. 10. George Adam Smith, in his great study of Isaiah, writes movingly on the theme. He pointed out that, in the East, poverty meant more than material deprivation. The poor man was too often in popular religion marked down as the God-forsaken, a humiliating and despairing conclusion to which he himself was too commonly driven. He was reft of justice, in consequence, of respect and acceptance. The condition coloured his thinking, and made him 'poor in spirit'. It was one of the results of the Exile, in which great and small, one-time rich and one-time poor, were mingled in misfortune (Isa. 24.1–5) that the Jews learned the deep lesson that affluence was no sign of God's approval, and poverty, far from being the mark of heaven's wrath, could be a path to God.

**19,20** The two verses are designed to form a stirring conclusion. Again and again man needs to learn the lesson of his helplessness and fragility. A slave stood beside the general, as he rode his chariot in a Roman triumph, whose function was to whisper to the great man in his greatest hour a reminder of his mere mortality. Life, and all around us and within, can be trusted to whisper that same reminder. And was this another verse Isaiah had in mind when he wrote his dramatic ending to the chapter already quoted (24.16–23)?

# 10

**Read Psalm 10**

### Occasion and author

This psalm is closely enough associated in theme and language with its predecessor, inevitably to prompt the suggestion that they form one poem. This by no means follows. The occasion of writing is obviously the same, or, amid life's common repetitions, a similar one. It seems also apparent that the author is the same. The juxtaposition may merely illustrate the habit of the editor of the psalms already noted. His intimate knowledge of the text of the Psalter led to a tendency to group according to language. It was not, in fact, a bad idea, for mnemonic considerations held weight with him. On the other hand the mood of the psalm is not identical. It is more sombre, less victorious, and begins with man's age-old perplexity before the strength of evil and the apparent silence of God.

### Commentary

**1** Here is Habakkuk's dilemma of evil prospering and the suffering of the innocent. Moffatt has some vigorous language in his translation of this psalm. God hides Himself 'in desperate hours', while 'the ungodly are haughty and harry the downtrodden' (1,2). It is an ancient dilemma on which Calvary alone throws light. If God in Christ ('reconciling the world to himself') suffered all that the cross signified, it is clear that there is meaning in the pain of good men which forms part of a great plan. God asks those who follow Him to look at Christ, and, like Habakkuk, 'live by faith' (or 'faithfulness' as some render) – the trust and inner certainty that in some final mystery they share in a process involving God Himself.

**2–6** It is difficult, none the less, for flesh so to endure. The psalmist is confronting evil, and paints an extraordinarily vigorous picture of a corrupt society with wicked men riding high. There is pride, persecution (2) and godless arrogance (3). The wicked boasts of the 'desires of his heart'. The phrase recurs in Psa. 37.4. It signifies the ultimate ambition of the human personality, the end to which the whole intention of the soul drives. For wickedness to be so intimately enthroned, to seep so completely into open speech and the thought which lies behind all words and expression, suggests reprobation and sin so dominant and victorious that something unpardonable, after the fashion of the Lord's reproach to the Pharisees, would seem to have taken place. The sinner of this verse plots evil, boasts of it, despises God and dismisses Him from all his thinking. The 'pride of his countenance' in Hebrew is pictorially expressed by 'the elevation of his nose', and a fine and energetic image of the loathsome rebel who scorns God equally with God's creatures. 'He thinks, in his insolence, "God never punishes"; his thoughts amount to this, "There is no God at all" ' (4,5, as Moffatt quaintly renders). The secret glee over apparent immunity soon moves to open atheism, a thought which immediately prompts the expression of complacency in v. 6. God's ways are beyond the shallow thinking of evil man. His mills grind slowly. Hence (6) the confidence of the sinner, a confidence which also shocked and shook Job.

In vs. 5 and 6 the Hebrew is described as 'gnarled and obscure'. The thought wavers between God and those who defy God. The psalmist could indeed be rendering the mood of the godly, trusting but disturbed, holding fast to the confidence that God is, God sees, God will requite, but none the less hurt and shaken at the immediate spectacle of sin so apparently triumphant. Habakkuk found the remedy in faith. Malachi found it in fellowship. There were those who said: ' "It is useless to serve God" and "What gain is it to do His bidding, to walk in penitent garb before the Lord of Hosts? It is the worldly, we find, who are well off; evildoers prosper, they dare God – and they escape!" ' (Mal. 3.14,15, Moffatt). But Malachi continues: 'So indeed they muttered. But meanwhile those who worshipped the Eternal talked to each other, and the Eternal heeded them and heard them . . .' (16).

**7–11** These verses repeat the desperation of the onlooker. He sees the victims, as anyone in this same world can see them today, innocent, helpless, meek, the subject of malediction and cheating, lies and slander (7), even murder and persecution (8). The world, as the psalmist's desperation saw it, was a jungle (9) with the feeble as helpless before vice and violence as a man unarmed before a wild and ravening beast (10). Amid the mounting crime of an urban world, modern eyes see a picture not unrecognizable. And it is all the fruit of godlessness.

**12–18** 'Often,' Abraham Lincoln once said, 'I am driven to my knees because there is nowhere else to go.' One divine and beneficent purpose is thereby served if abounding evil itself drives good men to prayer. This is precisely what happens in the movement of this psalm. Visibly, or perhaps the word is audibly, the writer breaks through to confidence. Prayer bursts out in an almost petulant cry with v. 12, moving passionately to reasoned appeal in the next three eloquent verses, quietens to an affirmation of faith in v. 16, and ends in quietness and confidence in the last two verses.

## Conclusion

Here then is a demonstration of prayer. An intolerable spectacle of evil overwhelms a good man, and, in the hot indignation of the moment, almost drives him to doubt the willingness of Eternal Holiness to act with power against massive evil. The situation grows clear with the spreading of the facts before God. Then, like the clearing of the vision of Elisha's manservant (2 Kings 6.15–17), the psalmist begins to assess the situation with a quieter and a more reverent mind. Like Peter on the water he can now see to whom he should strongly reach (Matt. 14.30,31). And as Malachi was led to see, as the passage quoted above moves on (17,18), all was in control. Meanwhile prayer has already fulfilled one function. It has led to heart-searching (Gen. 18.27) and demonstrated that its whole exercise is sometimes a desperate striving of the soul. 'Go on asking, go on knocking, go on seeking . . .' run the three present imperatives in the Lord's triple exhortation. We 'wrestle on towards heaven', as Anne Ross Cousin put it well, ''gainst storm and wind and tide', in the commonest experience. If any, as a lesser hymn would have it, go 'singing as they upward bound' the experience is both less common and less salutary.

# 11

**Read Psalm 11; 1 Samuel 18.5–16**

**Occasion and author**

This poignant little poem, like a long tract of the Psalter from the second psalm onwards, is ascribed to David. Failing the most compelling reasons for doubt, the tradition may be accepted, and in the succeeding studies, where venerable rabbinical ascription claims Davidic authorship, the claim will be allowed. That strange urge, so common in biblical scholarship, to question a traditional position simply because it is traditional, operates in no other sphere of ancient literature, and thought will be given to discovering the occasion rather than discussing the authorship.

Some time of trouble gave birth to these words. We have followed a sequence of psalms which seem to belong to a second period of literary activity inspired by Absalom's rebellion. This psalm can hardly refer to that period because the advice to withdraw to the friendly hill-country appears to be rejected in the opening verse, as a counsel of timidity. Perhaps the prayer dates from the tense days in Saul's court when it was becoming clear that a passionate and unbalanced man held authority, and that law, custom and old standards gave no protection to the good.

**Commentary**

**1** An affirmation of faith meets advice not without its attractiveness. 'Your mountain' (KJV, RSV margin) is the phrase of an anxious friend, 'fly, bird, to your mountain', literally . . . Perhaps the metaphor was David's own, or perhaps it remained in his mind, for there was an occasion when he reproached Saul for chasing him as one hunts a partridge in the hills (1 Sam. 26.20). The rugged hill-country was always a refuge for the outlaw, and the wilderness was in David's blood. The temptation to escape was strong, and if the next two verses are part of the persuasive plea of friends, the advantages of flight were real.

**2** In fact, treachery was afoot. There were those preparing 'to shoot in the dark at the upright in heart'. Their plans were mature. The bow was strong,

the arrow was fitted to the string. The weapon was bent. All that was required was the loosing of the shaft, the mere opening of finger and thumb which would leave the taut string and bent wood to speed the deadly missile against those whose hearts were clean. Good has always been the target of evil and we should not 'be surprised', as Peter said (1 Pet. 4.12).
**3** It required some grip and reach of faith to withstand the urge to flee. The Lord Himself sanctioned flight when drastic evil stood in seemingly absolute power, man's ultimate blasphemy in the holy place (Matt. 24.15–21). Society depends on moral foundations. By a mutual agreement which Rousseau called a 'social contract', man in an ordered and civilized society sets limits to his own conduct. When such obligations are repudiated and law collapses along with the order it brings, what option has the man who seeks peace? He can endure, suffer injustice, die in his integrity – or he can abandon the context of evil, if a place of refuge can be found. David found that he was compelled to retreat on more than one occasion. But not at the time of this imaginary conversation.
**4** The reply of the psalmist comes with v. 4. First let it be remembered that the Almighty is not dethroned nor blind to the wickedness of men. If He sees and abstains from punitive action, it is because He is fulfilling some remoter or wider purpose. Like Jeremiah observing the gush of blossom on the spring almond tree immediately before the horrifying vision of the overflowing cauldron of the north, David is convinced that history is not out of control. If God permits, God has His beneficent reason (Jer. 1.10–14).
**5** And not the least of those reasons could be, as this verse says, the strengthening of the faith of those prepared to trust, prepared to seek and prepared to understand (Hab. 2.1–4). The good man is tested and tried by the seeming inactivity of God, but he can rest in the thought that God must loathe evil and the violence to which evil, by its very nature, turns.
**6** That is why the memory of the cities of the Plain slips into the poet's mind. Those grim little towns of the great Rift Valley, steaming with their sin, found the earth and sky exploding round them. Gales swept down from the north in the deep cleft which cuts from the Lebanon Beqaa deep into Africa, but when the fires beneath the globe's deep wound themselves exploded, flinging out in fiery mass the very salt of forgotten seas, the tempest generated by the upsurging heat was a veritable rain and gale of fire and brimstone. Some vanished hand scrawled the words SODOMA GOMORA on a wall in Pompeii, perhaps on that August day of A.D. 79 when Vesuvius raised its mushroom cloud and blotted out the town. Some few, perhaps remembered what Abraham saw (Gen. 19.24–28) and interpreted it as Abraham did. The writer passed through the same sequence of thought. If God thus bent history to judgement, and thus delivered even those with some pretence to good, so now must He, in His good time, do again.

**Conclusion**

That is why the closing verse forms the full conclusion of the argument. His is no averted gaze. His face is full on the righteous man, and His follower can look up and meet Him eye to eye and drink in strength. As John Newton's hymn, already quoted, had it:

*Though dark be my way,*
*Since He is my Guide,*
*'Tis mine to obey,*
*'Tis His to provide;*
*Though cisterns be broken*
*And creatures all fail,*
*The word He hath spoken*
*Shall surely prevail.*

It is a fine conclusion to reach, but an act of faith which does not go unchallenged, as the next psalms seem to show. It was with some perception that the rabbis ordered and arranged them thus – unless indeed the order was determined long since in some primitive collection put biographically in place by the writer himself.

# 12

**Read Psalm 12; 1 Samuel 10.27; 26.17–20**

### Occasion and author

The tradition of Davidic authorship again need not be rejected. With his strong feeling for the past and its documents, a type of critical awareness which comes only with long and intimate association with a people's history and memorials, W. F. Albright wrote: 'There can be little doubt, in my opinion, that there are scores of psalms whose composition can be dated in the tenth century or shortly afterwards, and it becomes hypercritical to reject the tradition of Davidic sponsorship (which is tantamount to authorship at that early period) of a substantial nucleus of the present Book of Psalms.'

It was a characteristic of David's personality that he reacted with deep distress to treachery, slander and cynical falsehood. He himself was marked by a strong strain of unquestioning loyalty. He naturally expected the same from others and in general won it. The quality which no doubt contributed much to his personal charm, on the other hand, sometimes betrayed him. He met treachery and cried aloud against it in many of his psalms. The readings suggested above provide illustration.

Unlike its predecessor, however, this piece is not intensely personal. There is more of Wordsworth's 'emotion recollected in tranquillity' about it. It is written for the congregation, for one man's pain can be another's, and it is the function both of public prayer and the highest poetry to take that which has hurt and wounded one heart and for which, perhaps, healing has been found, and make the experience available in choice and memorable language to others.

**Commentary**

**1** The hyperbole is natural enough. In a dark mood of defeat it is a common delusion, as Elijah discovered in his loneliness, to think there are no others left who follow good and God. The Hebrew word for 'the faithful' is connected with the verb which means to trust, and the idea of truth haunts the meaning. 'Amen' is from the same root, and Luther translates the word quite literally *Amenleute* – 'Amenfolk'. These are they who give assent to the great spiritual realities, to God's virtues, to His perfect will. Did not Paul remark that utter dedication was the pathway to understanding the ultimate goodness, indeed the perfection, of the Lord's will (Rom. 12.1,2)?

**2** 'With lips of smoothness' (the phrase is almost the same in the polluted context of Prov. 7.21) the liars speak. Controlled and deliberate falsehood, graced by soft words, which carry conviction, is their mark. They have 'a heart and a heart', two personalities, one fabricated and presented falsely to the world, the other within, the true, corrupted self.

**3** The psalmist's indomitable faith is that God will deal with such offence in His good time. We have already quoted James Russell Lowell's poem. When truth seems ever in rout, and evil continually in triumph, faith in final justice is the only resort. The boast of little men, human arrogance and pride, ultimately incarnate in the apocalyptic Beast, shall wither before Omnipotent Reality. There is no other confidence available.

**4** 'Arrogance'? The human hosts of such disease are confident that they have powerful weapons in their lies. And who shall stop them from saying what they will? 'Our lips are with us,' they say. 'We can say what we will. Who is our master?' It is the mad cry of Psa. 2. again, with little man uplifted against Almighty God.

**5** With a shift of imaginative thought, the poet sees God rise to deal with such wickedness. 'The poor and needy' have no other protection. They long for justice and shall receive it. Such consummation still tarries. Such a mood often sweeps the conscience of the Church at the spectacle of man's intolerance and cruelty to man. Ebenezer Elliott, a Sheffield man, who was in the thick of the battle for the repeal of the Corn Laws in the forties of the last century, wrote a hymn which is still sung:

*When wilt Thou save the people,*
*O God of mercy, when?*
*Not kings alone but nations,*
*Not thrones and crowns, but men!*

It is part of the incomparable Isaiah's closing visions. It is still part of the heart's cry.

**6** And the promise stands . . . like pure silver. Silver in the Old Testament is a metal often given priority over gold. The refining processes of the time produced a pure metal, and the psalmist pictures the operation seven times repeated. Silver does not tarnish if the atmosphere is pure, and the word of God so stands in the heart prepared to accept it. The meaning of the verse is a little obscure and 'on the ground' seems vague. Is the phrase a remnant of an ancient gloss which has strayed into the text, or is it, as Maclaren suggests, a picture of the molten metal, free from dross, running down glittering into the mould on the ground – a fine figure of the pure word of God running into the poor container of the human spirit?

**7** Hence confidence. 'Man's clouded sun shall brightly rise', as Elliott's hymn continues, 'And songs ascend instead of sighs.' But when? We can only repeat the words with which the Bible itself ends: 'Even so, come, Lord Jesus.'

**8** And that is how the psalm might have ended. Why then the sudden reversion in the last verse? That is how the mind works. The suppliant rises from his knees and the world is still there. He opens his eyes, and Masefield's vision of the city street is still visible, 'the king's face, and the cur's face, and the face of the stuffed swine'. In the human scene much is upside down. There is dramatic reality in the ending. The psalmist, for all that one feels, faces it now, strengthened, fortified. He is back on earth, but he has come from the presence of the Most High.

**Read Psalm 13**

### Occasion and author

Perhaps this little prayer compresses much experience. It may be an utterance of the hunted days of the Judean wilderness, when the burden of exile and deprivation seemed endless, and many a day was like the day of this battle of the soul. It is perhaps a memory, for the pattern of the verse is ordered though passionate. Three strophes of equal length show the transition from intense agitation to the calm of trust.

### Commentary

**1** 'How long?' is a question four times repeated . . .

*Out of the depths I cry, How long*
*Must I taste the gall of the cup of wrong,*
*And lose the lilt of life's marching song,*
*When the light of the day is done?*

**2** The first half of the verse seems to refer to the night, and the Septuagint actually inserts the word to balance the phrase 'all the day' in the corresponding portion of the antithetical rhythm. Apparently abandoned, what can a man do but eat his soul away? It is one of the sternest tests of faith when God appears not to care, to be inactive, dead.

**3** The passionate questioning of the first strophe calms itself in the second, and as though by stern effort puts the substance of the complaint into words. David yearns for some taste of victory on his parched soul, some shred of hope. Dying eyes are glazed, and he feels the breath of death upon him.

**4** And why? Saul was mad, or bad, or both, and the world had gone after Saul. Wrong was again on the throne and God forgotten. It was bitter to the soul to hear the triumphant words of evil, and surely such victory, such boasting, could not be the will of a holy God? The suppliant longs for the the sustenance of vindication. He is 'shaken', admits it, and writhes that the one who shook his faith should make a boast of it.

**5** And then, as though the very putting of his pain into words had brought the answer and the healing, the mood changes to confidence. Unseen, God has done something, touched a core of old confidence, and quietened distress.

**6** He has what he needed – a trust renewed in God's steadfastness, God's salvation. He can say, 'life's marching song' is on his lips again and the reach of faith can utter praise for bounty, rich giving from the One who, in the psalm's wild opening, was almost the theme of reproach.

**Conclusion**

This is a cameo of experience. The writer has known the flash of sun after thunder, the benison of prayer when darkness seems eternal. The reversal which forms the theme, the transformation wrought, could have been a longer procession in the reality of events, than in the brevity of their expression. It is good, however, to see in short conspectus the beginning, and the middle, and the end.

# 14

**Read Psalm 14; Micah 3**

## Introduction

Maclaren notes some similarity of situation between this psalm and Pss. 10 and 12. 'We have three psalms,' he remarks, 'closely connected but separated from each other by Pss. 11 and 13. Now it is observable that these three have no personal references, and that the two which part them have. It would appear that the five are arranged on the principle of alternating a general complaint on the evil of the times with a more personal pleading of an individual sufferer.' He also observes that these five psalms – 'a little group of wailing and sighs' – are marked off from those before them and those which come after by two poems of an entirely different tone: Pss. 9 and 15.

His remark is perceptive and raises a subject of some interest. Why did the final editor or editors of the Psalter arrange the contents in the familiar order? There are many motives – similarity in tone, historical connection, authorship, linkage of vocabulary and theme . . . all of which will aid understanding and bring the reader closer to the minds of devoted men who can claim to have been the world's first great Bible scholars.

## Occasion and author

The tradition of authorship, failing reasons legitimately to question it, is again accepted. The theme is again general, like that of Psa. 12. It is comment generalized from bitter and wounding experience, but not necessarily remote from it. Alive to the darker colours of humanity, the writer sees society in sombre colours. If a distinction is to be drawn with Psa. 12, it is that deeds here, words there, dominate the picture. The poem is tense and dramatic.

## Commentary

**1** Taking a shorter and more immediate view of history the shallow thinker doubts the reality of the moral government of the world, concludes in that inner forum of the spirit, where action finds root, that impunity is sure, and proceeds accordingly. When no moral authority exists, when no ultimate judgement is to be feared, it is natural enough that, in person and society, standards crumble and morality collapses. A conclusion proceeds to an action. In his essay on atheism, Francis Bacon suggests a slight psychological twist. Corrupt action is chosen as a path of life, and then, to remove discomfort or the twinge of conscience, the wicked man 'saith by rote to himself what he would have, rather than what he can thoroughly believe.' We may have this view or that, or a mingling of both. Was it not Thomas Huxley who admitted, for all his atheism, that man 'functions better' when he believes in God? And Browning's word, put in Bishop Blougram's mouth, is well known. No man who expels God from his thinking can be secure. He, too, ironically enough, lives by faith, and all the material advantages of 'abominable doings' cannot always quench the surge of doubt.

**2** A dramatic three verses picture God's contemplation of earth's scene. It is only in the knowledge of this vast awareness that man can face life, and the fragility of that faith was David's constant problem.

**3** 'See,' said Luther, 'how many words he uses that he may comprehend all, excluding none. First he says *all*, then *together*, and then *no, not one*.' Paul's use of a free rendering in Rom. 3.10 is well known. A concern seems to haunt the verse. 'No care, Lord, hast Thou', of W. C. Smith's hymn is far from the truth, if God is to be seen in Christ, sorrowing, yearning over His people.

**4** God speaks in this vivid drama of His contemplation, and speaks in judgement. Ignorance, culpable, self-chosen, and dumb disregard of God, spawn oppression – a thought which Micah develops with strong and violent imagery (3.1–3). Common men, the helpless, the poor, are in peril when godlessness holds authority.

**5** The scene shifts to earth and like some picture of the judged from the Apocalypse, the evil of the world discover that God was a member of the race they had oppressed – 'the generation of the righteous'.

**6** And in that confidence the psalmist who has staged the drama turns to address the miscreants who have sought to organize society as if God did not exist. There emerges the dominant concept of the Old Testament, the God of justice and righteousness – no 'surly tapster' of Fitzgerald's Omar, nor an indulgent parent of others' equally fallible imagination, but the Holy One who cannot abide cruelty, oppression and man's inhumanity to man.

**7** In the KJV, this verse, like the closing verses of Psa. 51, looks like a liturgical addition, no clumsy ending but an adaptation of a Davidic poem to the worship of the Temple of which the Psalter is the Prayer Book. That is why this closing verse cannot with any likelihood be used to date the psalm in post-exilic times. There is no reason why devotion should not append such prayers, nor indeed why their words should not be accorded reverence. Daniel turned in prayer towards Jerusalem (6.10f.) and the Psalter took shape and form in the days of deprivation when the Word of God alone took new meaning in the scattered community of Israel. Jerusalem became a symbol of restoration, the resumption of a destiny and a task of witness begun again.

Kidner, however, supporting the RSV and NEB, would fuse v.7 more intimately with the rest, and invalidate the suggestion that it is a liturgical appendage. 'There is general support,' he says, 'for the rendering *restores the fortunes* (or well-being), which is more comprehensive' (*Tyndale Old Testament Commentaries – Psalms, p. 80*). As Derek Kidner points out, 'the Christian is taught by Rom. 8.19–25 to pray such a prayer in the context of the whole creation's "eager longing" for liberty.'

# 15

**Read Psalm 15; 2 Samuel 6.12–19**

**Occasion and author**

This small hymn could have been written for the same purpose as that which inspired Psa. 24 – the restoration of the Ark to Zion and the consecration there of some tent or dwelling place. 'Who shall sojourn in thy tent? Who shall dwell on thy holy hill?', is a pointer to some great restoration of public worship. The placing of the psalm at this point may have been to point a contrast with the darker denizens of corruption who haunt the psalm which goes before. It comes like sunshine after thunder. Like the Lord's Prayer, the psalm opens with a plea to God whose presence pervades all five verses.

**Commentary**

**1** The tent was always the symbol of Israel's deliverance. It stood for the days of independence which formed their nation in the wilderness. Abraham had abandoned city life and sought to found in the desert a new clean nation, dedicated to God, '. . . living in tents with Isaac and Jacob,' as Hebrews puts it. 'To your tents, O Israel' was the nation's rallying cry, and the Festival of Tents annually reminded the people of their past. And when Israel, battered but welded, emerged from Egypt, a tent was a tool of God's instruction. Chapter after chapter in the story, following the vivid narrative of a disastrous lapse into idolatry, tell of the construction of a beautiful tent. What was its object? The message was this. God dwelt among His people, not as a graven image, but as an unseen presence, symbolized by the empty throne above the mercy-seat. His tent was buffeted by the desert winds which strained at the goatskin covers of the multitude. The same sun beat down on it. John says exquisitely that Christ, in the flesh, 'tabernacled among us', and opens a world of thought. In a kind of spiritual poem, the Tabernacle pictured the Presence, which was to be, and was. It was built by gift and sacrifice, it spoke of blood shed for sin.

**2** The question has been asked. Dramatically the psalmist gives God's answer, a kind of Decalogue of conduct, for there are ten marks of the upright man in the next four verses . . . The Hebrew is stronger than some versions. *Tamim* is something wider than 'blameless'. The word is used of 'God's way' in Psa. 18.30. It contains the ideas of soundness, wholesomeness, integrity. Such a man is healthy. His presence does not pollute this environment. He does not infect others with evil. He cannot but 'do righteousness', as the text goes on to say. The KJV is closer to the original than the RSV here. And since the root of all upright character and righteous action is the core of the personality, such as 'speaks truth from his heart', not with 'a lick of the tongue', as Bunyan put it, but in words which emerge sincerely from the sanctified person.

**3** The verse passes to three specific spheres of action. Again the psalmist reverts to his preoccupation with evil done to another in treachery, mendacity and spite. One can injure by word, by deed or by disloyally listening. The last mark of the true man is worth attention; 'Love covers up', as both Proverbs (10.12) and Paul (1 Cor. 13.7) insist.

**4** Such a man, in fact, despises the doer of evil. Abraham's very proper scorn of the reprobate chieftain of the vile little towns of Sodom and Gomorrah is a perfect illustration of this quality of dignified aloofness (Gen. 14.17–24). Nothing is said of the 'reprobate's' wealth or social standing. He, like 'those who fear the Lord' in the antithetical sequence of the verse, is judged, rejected or accepted purely on the grounds of moral worth, with no thought of the normal standards of worldly judgement. Such a man does not waver. He stands by his undertakings even when he finds his plighted word involves him in damaging and unexpected loss.

**5** That is why the good man avoids unworthy or perilous modes of life. Money-lending can involve the lender in situations damaging to integrity. The Old Testament is suspicious of 'usury' (Lev. 25.35–38; Deut. 23.19), and a good man, conscious of the weakness of human nature, alert to circumvent the possibility of temptation, and setting store by his personal integrity and testimony will avoid profession, trade or practice which contains such dangers.

**Conclusion**

H. S. Perowne sums up well: 'Such is the figure of stainless honour drawn by the Jewish poet. Christian chivalry has not dreamed of a greater. We have need often and seriously to ponder it, for it shows us that faith in God and spotless integrity may not be sundered; that religion does not veil or excuse petty dishonesties; that love to God is only then worthy the name when it is the life and bond of every social virtue. Every line is a touchstone to which we should bring ourselves . . .'

# 16

**Read Psalm 16; Matthew 11.28–30**

**Occasion and author**

Some high peak of faith and ardour in David's life inspired this exquisite expression of devotion. Perhaps we are again in the context of the wilderness when the patrols of Saul hunted their future king amid the ravines and wild uplands of the Judean hill-country.

**Commentary**

**1** It is a perilous world. 'Deliver us from evil' has many forms and connotations. No evil dwells in God and the final safety is in His keeping.

**2** Hence the words of committal which follow. There are no alternatives to complete consecration (Rom. 12.1,2). The verse is brief and cryptic, and from the Septuagint and the Vulgate onwards a variety of renderings have been offered. Major modern versions follow the simplicity of the RSV: 'I have no good apart from thee.' Compare Moffatt: 'My welfare rests on thee alone.'

**3** Those who thus trust are a mighty fellowship, the land's true nobility, earth's salt. There is a touch of pathos in the word, if indeed this asseveration of faith came from the days of loneliness when David needed Elijah's assurance that there were others too 'who had not bowed to Baal'.

**4** As though he remembered that very story, the suppliant turns in horror on the bloodthirsty gods of paganism. The haunting evil of human sacrifice runs from Jericho to Carthage where the archaeologists of Tunis, anticipating suburban development, examine ancient Phoenician cemeteries and discover the charred remains of infants, sacrificed to Moloch. The deity a person worships, true or false, makes a mark on the character of the worshipper. Hence the fierce denunciations of the prophets against the gods of the groves, the baals of the fields, and other objects of licentious fertility cults. The tragedy of poor Hosea's life was the absorption of his weak wife's person by some such evil. The verse alludes to the Fall. The word to Eve was almost identical with the sinister phrase 'multiply sorrow' (Gen. 3.16). 'Choose', too, is a powerful word. The psalmist believes that man is free to bestow his ultimate loyalty and that is the awesome truth.

**5** Like Joshua taking his stand without a moment's pause to observe the movement of his audience (Josh. 24.15), he announces his firm resolve. He chooses, occupies and enjoys, for so the succeeding figures, 'chosen portion', 'cup', imply, and God confirms and establishes the choice. Taylor aptly paraphrases: 'The Lord himself is my inheritance, my prize. He is my food and drink, my highest joy! He guards all that is mine.'

**6** In imagery almost anticipating Psa. 23, David imagines his heritage in God like some choice portion of the land allotted in the settlement of the tribes. His boundary lines included 'pleasant pastures' and 'still waters'.

**7** And more – there is a Presence in the place, One who counsels and forms the patterns of thought in the stillness of the night, a Living One, closer than the beating heart, who permeates the surrendered personality and fills it with His life.

**8** God is real, like the friend who walks on the right hand and guards the sword-arm with His shield.

**9** Hence the deepest of inward joy, and confidence that safety will be his in the midst of menace.

**10** In the forward surge of his inspiration David seems to break through to truth only shadowy in its Old Testament expression. He suddenly senses the illogicality of death. There must be something more. Peter catches up this verse in his sermon on the Day of Pentecost, and shows that, unrealized in David, it became true in Christ; a metaphor in the psalm, it proved literal in history.

**11** But meanwhile there was a nearer life to live, and God's guidance alone could keep man's feet on the path, or God, to be more precise, in eternal companionship, would guide. Travelling directions fall short of an escort.

**Conclusion**

The theme, reaching its high points in vs. 1, 7, 8 and 11, is the nearness of Almighty God to the soul which trusts Him. It is the assurance which anxious man most longs for: 'Behold, I am with you always . . .' 'Where two or three are gathered . . .', and as a papyrus of Christ's sayings adds, 'and where one is alone I am there . . .' 'Break the stone and there thou wilt find me, cleave the wood and there I am . . .' Shelter, sanctification, safety, hang on the thought. Origen quotes a saying of Christ: 'He who is near me is near the fire', and in His enfolding presence the base dross of life is purged away. Such a consciousness leads naturally to a wider faith than this brief life can hold. In comfort and prosperity man finds his horizon narrow. When the way darkens, the old yearning for something more, for ultimate justice, the thirst, in a word, for life, emerges. It haunts hymnology – 'I shall see Him face to face . . .' 'That will be glory for me . . .' 'No sorrow yonder . . .' It is moving to find this ancient poem stirred by the same impulse.

# 17

## Read Psalm 17

### Occasion and author

The traditional authorship is again acceptable. The time of writing must have been in days of innocence and trouble which were the pattern of David's young manhood. The place in the collection was no doubt determined by a similarity of theme with the preceding psalm, and a contrast with the triumph of the great psalm which follows.

### Commentary

**1,2** A certain self-righteousness has been alleged in these verses but the charge crumbles in the context. We saw in Psa. 5 David's preoccupation with spiritual preparation for the presence of the Most High. The Lord's Prayer dictates such exercise of soul. This prayer presupposes it. David has made the necessary self-examination. In the processes of the Law, certain rituals expedited the conviction of innocence. Two other points may be considered. First, the conscience of man had not yet been presented with the perfection of Christ. Second, Maclaren's comment is worth a glance: 'The modern type of religion which recoils from such professions, and contents itself with always confessing sins which it has given up hope of overcoming, would be all the better for listening to the psalmist and aiming a little more vigorously and hopefully at being able to say, "I know nothing against myself".' That robust word has an air of finality about it.

**3–6** The claim has not been hasty. The words have been measured. The suppliant has lain awake at night and used the time of solitude and quietness to search his soul in God's presence. Even when accused of lies and violence, and the suspicion that these had been unjust charges levelled against the suppliant, he claims to have guarded his lips and trodden firmly in the paths of good. That is why, with a clean heart and no stain upon his mind, he feels free to call for vindication.

**7–12** He calls for some token of God's love, some strengthening manifestation of God's concern and God's care. Like the swift reflex action of the eyelids which protect the precious eye from damage, he trusts that God will shield and shelter him. Like the eagle's chick of Moses' word picture, he hides under mighty wings (Deut. 32.11). With v. 10 the memories crowd in of the beleaguered days. It is like a vision of the night with gusts of anger (10) against the well-fed men of the royal rangers, tracking down the elusive outlaws of the rocky wadis (11), scanning every nook and cliffside cave (11), skilfully setting ambush like lions about to pounce (12). Might is like that for those who live in fear and tension. David could not afford to sleep deeply. The enemy was too near, too enveloping. The three verses (10–12) are a vivid little picture of what the imagination did when composure (3) momentarily snapped and the sounds in the darkness took on sinister meaning.

**13,14** How he needed allies, a sword beside him. And how the venial minions of Saul merited the judgement of God. The aggressive tone of this prayer may be pre-Christian, but the suppliant, holding in desperate faith to his call, saw the conspiracy against him as a flouting of the will of God. The petition contains no personal rancour, and must be seen in the light of one concerned for Israel, the land's divine destiny and the ordered government under God which was the requisite for this.

**15** Various lame interpretations of this verse have arisen from the preconceived idea that faith in a resurrection was not held in Israel at this time. This is much too arbitrary a base for interpretation. It would be difficult to discover a people whose records in any form survive, which had no ideas of another mode of existence beyond death. It is not to be supposed that a people with a lofty monotheism at the heart of their religion should lack all conception of resurrection and survival, for all the reticence of the Old Testament on the theme. In fact there is much that points at least to a nascent faith in a resurrection. The strange vision of Ezekiel of the dead in a valley plain, the sad remnants of some garrison overrun by the Babylonian armour, could have little meaning among people quite without concept of a resurrection. The wild 'taunt song' of Isaiah's fourteenth chapter, in which a dead tyrant joins the ironic dead, is not the poetry of those who had no notion of a conscious existence after death. To be sure, the idea of resurrection may have taken deeper hold on minds stirred to hope and faith by the agony of exile, but that is no argument for dating passages of literature on such assumption, and certainly the exiles, abhorring the paganism which flowed round their misery, would not have been likely to absorb ideas from Babylonian mythology. The idea of survival was there, an emerging faith, long before the trauma of tyranny and deportation. The close of this psalm surely speaks of communion with God deeper than that of mortality with deity. The closing verse of the next psalm suggests the same hope. So do 49.15 and 73.24. Psa. 73, in fact, seems to reach out to the triumphant words of Paul in Rom. 8, linking the Testaments in the thought that death cannot separate God and His redeemed.

# 18

**Read Psalm 18**

### Occasion and author

The Davidic authorship and the occasion are attested in 2 Sam. 22, where the poem is set out as a summary of David's life. Perhaps it was the royal poet's favourite hymn, written long before, in the early joy of his triumph, and recalling to him in darker days the experience which had once been his before the brightness of his life was hazed by his own sad fall, and the troubles which came from it. Apart from this historical attestation, the internal evidence of authorship is clear enough. The daring imagery, the vigour of language, the ardour of devotion are David's; the biographical thread which may be disengaged from the whole vigorous poem fits the facts of the king's life.

### Commentary

**1,2** The word for love is a strong and vivid one, found in this form only here in the Hebrew Scriptures. Luther was correct in translating: 'Herzlich lieb habe ich dich . . .' – 'from my heart I love you . . .' Religion is too cold a word for such devotion. David touches here the summit of the soul's experience of God. They are strong words, too, for 'rock' and 'fortress'. The former word is like the New Testament *petra*, the 'crag' on which the wise man set his house, and on which Christ was to build His Church. It was a word applied to Petra, the rock city of the Nabateans – the 'rose red city, half as old as time'. The second word is the base of the name applied to the famous stronghold by the Dead Sea, Masada, a symbol in Israeli minds for an enduring defiance of vicious assault. The imagery is built out of the Judean wilderness where David saw the strength of his God in the enfolding landscape, the shielding power of the stark crags and outcrops where God, he felt, had hidden him.

**3** That is why he telescopes those years of glad health and faith in one verse. Taylor's paraphrase touches the feeling of the verse: 'All I need to do is cry to him – oh, praise the Lord – and I am saved from all my enemies!'

**4–6** These verses elaborate. Verse 4 is quoted at Acts 2.24, in the Greek Septuagint rendering, and the phrase reads 'the travailings of death' – as though out of life was to emerge in agony life's last antithesis, the final enemy – Death. In the version given in 2 Samuel, the figure is different and consistent rather with the furious imagery of storm into which the poem is about to break. It is 'the billows of death' – the wave on wave onslaught of a heavy sea. 'Then in anguish of heart,' as the NEB puts it, 'I cried to the Lord . . .' And God heard, the verse ends, 'from his temple'. The words, of course, mean the sky, the blue dome of heaven, our linguistic symbol for the 'dwelling-place of God'. Even the Roman Epicurean poet Lucretius can call the space above us *templa serena* – 'the region of peace'. Why should David be accused of locating his God in the place where the ark was stored in Jerusalem?

**7–15** These verses should be read in one sweep, and not analysed. They are a poem of storm, and typical of much poetry outside the classical tradition. Modern poetry is frequently of this order, a tumult of imagery and interlocking metaphor. David has in his memory the splendid terror of a storm in the rugged Judean hills. Flash floods and downpour were common there. That is how Masada retained its water supply during the three-year siege. It may have been a tempest of rain and wind of the sort which follow a seismic disturbance. Lightning stabbed, the wild wadis filled and gushed with torrential water, the winds howled, funnelled down the Great Rift Valley, itself an ancient earthquake fault. The cloud ceiling dropped and the wild updraughts from the gales, caught and tangled in the deep ravines, drove the cloud streamers upward. Hence the bold imagery of v. 8, misunderstood by prosaic theologians and avid literary critics as a descent into anthropomorphism, or some form of Baal Storm-God worship. The whole fierce picture is quite magnificent. Drenched and buffeted, perhaps even struggling in the flooded valley floor, David exulted in it all. It was like life, a confrontation and a matching of strength between a puny man and elemental forces, with puny man so much the greater because he could think.

**16–19** From such a tempest God delivered him. He had felt the majesty of God in the tumult of the heavens. It was not a 'theophany', as Maclaren terms it, any more than a visible appearance of God Almighty is envisaged when we sing:

*His chariots of wrath*
*The deep thunder-clouds form,*
*And dark is His path*
*On the wings of the storm . . .*

But the swift, coloured imagery dies out with v. 17 and the mere fact of deliverance is stressed. Maclaren's comment is now perceptive; 'The outside of a fact is not all of it; and in this mystical life of ours poetry gets nearer to the heart of things than does prose, and religion nearer than either . . . his eye has seen the unseen force which moves all visible things . . .' 'The gale of life', to use Housman's phrase from *Wenlock Edge*, had blown high, but the strong arm of God had brought David through to a 'place of liberty'.

**20–24** We have commented before on the claim to righteousness which appears often in the Davidic psalms, and which jars a little on a Christian. Consideration of the context is necessary – and for ourselves perhaps a little more vigour in claiming victory. Note, too, at the end of the psalm (31–50), the clear ascription of all strength, victory, protection to God. David comes near to the Christian position in 1 Cor. 1.30. Nor as v. 23 clearly enough states, was David unaware of attendant sin. He knew his weakness and stood on guard – words which must have lashed his heart in the day of his great moral disaster.

**25–27** Principles, indeed, emerge. Man chooses the pattern of his life. He can have of God what he will, being man, free to select his way, be it of obedience or of rebellion. Nor, as v. 24 observes, may God be outwitted. He is not ultimately mocked, as Paul pointed out to the Galatians (6.7).

**28–45** The theme turns to biography, and to the adventures of the wilderness. The picture emerges of a young warrior, exultant in his strength, strangely enjoying the challenge of peril, glorying in the play of firm muscles and lithe limbs. In fact, something in him looked back on those hunted days as the great days of true happiness, clean, free, bracing. Robert Browning, who liked muscular faith, had this psalm in mind when he made David reminisce in his *Saul*.

*Oh, our manhood's prime vigour! No spirit feels waste,*
*Not a muscle is stopped in its playing nor sinew unbraced.*
*Oh, the wild joys of living! The leaping from rock to rock.*
*The strong rending of boughs from the fir-tree, the cool silver shock*
*Of the plunge in a pool's living water, the hunt of the bear,*
*And the sultriness showing the lion is couched in his lair.*
*And the meal, the rich dates yellowed over with gold-dust divine . . .*

Perhaps there were times when the poet's soul panted for the scent of the hot rocks, the grit beneath the bearskin . . . The cloying comfort of the palace, the stifling court, adulation, the city, were no substitute. Those are sometimes the best days of life when circumstance challenges: 'Up now and wrestle. Try your strength on me . . .' And note that this is no exulting in an 'unconquerable soul' after the fashion of poor Henley's *Invictus*. The whole rich passage of testimony and triumph is laced through and through with the expression of a faith. He stands before men, and bows the knee to God, who gave him 'room to move, and a foothold sure' (36, Moffatt).

**46–50** A concluding paean of praise ends the psalm. He has been delivered from 'men of violence' (48). The word strikes hard in this hard world where every day sees the weak, the gentle, the defenceless made the prey of the mailed fist, the men of blood, the sword-swingers. They have cursed the world. It is the 'gentle', the 'meek' if you will, who are to inherit the earth, and on this note the Christian joins the psalmist in his prayer.

**Conclusion**

The psalm concludes itself. There are few higher expressions of personal faith, of strong conviction in right's ultimate victory, and of the blessedness of complete trust all woven into some of the greatest of Hebrew poetry. 'Life,' said Kierkegaard, 'can only be understood backward, but it must be lived forward.' This is the summary of a life, embattled, imperilled, but lived ardently, bravely and in faith. There is something terribly poignant in the evident fact that David held fast to these words he had himself written, till the shadowed evening of his life – if that is what the repeated version in the historical book really signifies.

# 19

**Read Psalms 8 and 19**

## Occasion and author

The rabbis attributed the whole cluster of psalms round this point in the Psalter to their poet king. The style, too, is congruent. This is a morning meditation, and one might imagine it to be a song of the Judean wilderness. Awake on some crag in the cool of the morning, the singer looks east, sees the pale silver blade of the Dead Sea and the deep purple of the Moab range. The opal sky above turns golden and with one leap comes the sun – like an eager youth away to claim his bride (5), or a runner springing from the mark. Dull critics, with no ear for poetry have seen 'sun worship' in the figure, some Baal remnant in Israel's thought. As well charge Coleridge (or his Ancient Mariner) with the notion:

*Nor dim nor red, like God's own head,*
*The glorious sun uprist.*

Entranced by the spectacle of precision, power, tremendous beauty, the psalmist thinks of the laws of God. The dusty commentators, arguing interpretation from arbitrary fixation of unverifiable dates, propose to date the psalm in Ezra's time when, it is alleged, the Law became a preoccupation. Alternatively, divide the psalm! What is more natural than that the beauty of nature to which David was uncommonly sensitive (Pss. 8 and 18 for example) should turn the mind to the beauty of holiness?

## Commentary

**1–6** Silent as light, the celestial pageant unfolds. 'There is no speech,' says v. 3, 'nor are there words; their voice is not heard.' Said Addison:

*What though in solemn silence all*
*Move round this dark terrestrial ball?*
*In reason's ear they all rejoice,*
*And utter forth a glorious voice.*

In the last psalm the skies shouted in tumult. Here they utter no word as their pageantry of precision and ordered movement speak to the whole world. The whole world is their territory, measured out for them (4) and coterminous with the sun. The silent moving host of heaven speaks, without words, of the Mind behind creation. As Paul told the Lystrans, the Athenians and the Romans, God's demonstration of His presence and His mind is in all He does.

**7–10** The thought of order, and the law which order presupposes, moves the mind naturally to order in the moral world.' Let our *ordered* lives confess,' said Whittier, 'the beauty of thy peace.' Whittier's poem (*The Brewing of Soma*) of which the last few verses form a well-known hymn, and of which the first nineteen are seldom quoted, is a protest against the disorders of a drug-cult. The Christian, the worshipper of a God of order, winds discipline into holiness. 'The starry heavens above,' said Kant, 'and the moral law within' turn the properly attuned mind to thoughts of awe. Hence the sequence of thought here. The psalmist passes from one witness to another. This is not to claim that his verses were not polished in tranquillity, for no better example of Hebrew poetic parallelism could well be found. Synonyms abound in noun, adjective and verb. They are the necessary verbal building bricks of this type of balanced poetry. The passage resembles the great psalm of the Word (119). The links with the first verses are obvious. The law of the Lord 'revives the soul' (RSV), 'renews life' (An American Translation – Smith, Goodspeed) – like the first beams of the sun in the fresh morning (7). 'The commandment of the Lord shines clear and gives light to the eyes' (8, NEB) – like the day's glory filling anew the bowl of the sky and sharpening every line of the land.

**11–14** The line of thought turns inward. The law is apprehended in the life, finds its illustration in experience, and like grace, must link with faith to be active. That is why a penetrating prayer of penitence and supplication closes the psalm. Verse 12 touches Christian doctrine. The suppliant yearns to be justified in God's eyes, purged of secret weakness and rescued from bolder and more visible sin (12,13). Verse 13 seems to show an awareness of moral peril of a specific but undefined nature. Did David, like all who examine themselves sincerely, know the weak places in the walls of life, the points where the Tempter presses hard, and where all that matters most is in danger? At such places let God guard.

**Conclusion**

In imagination or reality the suppliant rises from his knees. We all know, in private and in public prayer, how inadequate are our words, how imperfect the thought that finds its partial expression in them. We cannot know tomorrow. We do not know in full the moment and the day. We can only pray that God will answer the words we would use could we know as we are known, could we but see the shape of tomorrow, and understand as only Perfect Wisdom can. His Spirit, says Paul, prays for us in words which find no expression in the formal syllables of speech. Hence the closing verse.

# 20

**Read Psalm 20; 2 Samuel 10.1–12**

## Occasion and author

If this psalm was not written by David, it was written, at least, for him. It is coupled in the collection, as will be apparent, with the next psalm. Both are liturgical, and are placed at this point to break the sequence of more personal hymns. The king is about to go out to battle, and such occasions were not infrequent in David's life. They are still common enough behind those frontiers of strife. The psalm is an utterance for public worship in which the people invoke God's blessing on their king, the king replies, and the people close. Picture, in both these psalms, the pageantry in the place of worship, and imagine the sound of music as the Levites chant responsively.

## Commentary

**1–5** The people pray as the royal soldier sets out to meet the enemy, perhaps the Syrians who tended to out-number Israel in chariotry and cavalry (7). It is a fine, rich hymn, full of courage but courage born of faith. 'The God of Jacob' may be the chosen appellation because of a remembered word of the patriarch who, announcing Bethel as the goal of his march, said: 'I will make there an altar to the God who answered me in the day of my distress and has been with me wherever I have gone.' The sacrifices of prayer have been made, obligations fulfilled, and the theme rises in crescendo to affirmation of victory won and celebrated (5).

**6–8** Dramatically a single voice takes up the invocation. It could have been the king himself; it could have been a Levite with a fine voice like the *choregos* of the Greek dramatic chorus. The theme is bold acceptance of the people's faith. The royal leader has drawn strength from the loyalty and loving regard of those who have prayed for him. The chariots might roll down from Damascus over the level land on the Golan Heights, but an invisible host rode beside the king who 'trusted in the Lord his God'.

**9** The people round off the psalm in a loud cry of affirmation. An anthem closes the prayer. 'God save the king', is the rendering in the Septuagint and the Vulgate, the two most ancient of all translations, and there seems no need to depart from it. A later punctuation gave the rendering adopted by the KJV and NEB.

## Conclusion

The place of worship empties, and with measured tread, the clop of horses, the rolling of chariot wheels, the army marches out of Jerusalem. Will the weary repetitions of man's history never cease? Darkness fell and the long wait began. In small homes hearts were heavy, women lonely and children large-eyed with apprehension.

# 21

**Read Psalm 21; 2 Samuel 10.13–19**

### Occasion and author

Was it weeks, was it months, before the army marched back? It seemed years to some, but they came back, those who came back, with victory, and those who still could sing were gathered to render thanks for vast deliverance. We have noted in some of the early psalms of Absalom's rebellion the links between words and phrases from poem to poem. Note the same phenomenon of language here. Verse 2 of this psalm echoes v. 4 of its predecessor.

### Commentary

**1–6** The choir speak for the king, returned in triumph, the nation saved, prayer answered. The outcome is ascribed to God, as 20.7 promised. Intershot with the glad acknowledgement is the thought of a mysterious posterity (4). To be sure, it was common Eastern hyperbole to pray that a king might live forever (1 Kings 1.31; Neh. 2.3), and the form of words is not unknown in other psalms (23.6; 61.6; 91.16). However, from rabbinical to Christian interpreters, the thought of 'David's Greater Son', the Messiah, is found in the prayer.

**7–12** The singer addresses the king more intimately, in the second person. Victory won is a token and foretaste of triumphs yet to be. The words take flame in envisaging victory, aggressors driven like chaff and treachery recoiling on its inventors (11). Verse 9 runs literally 'at the time of your face', that is, 'when you appear', and the echo is found in Rev. 6.16, and perhaps in 2 Thess. 1.9. It is hot language, from which a war-ridden world may shrink, but see it in the context of an embattled land, with enemies like those which fill the sanguinary art and proclamations of the Assyrian and Babylonian conquerors yet to be. An appalling tradition of evil, international vendetta, can go on for centuries, and v. 10 must be read in that context of ever-breeding agony.

**13** The conclusion rescues the psalm from the spirit which could wrongly be seen in it by those insensitive to a beleaguered people's fear. It is God's strength, His power, that is exalted. Man recedes and God remains. Has any nation any other hope?

# 22

**Read Psalm 22; Mark 15.27–34**

**Occasion and author**

While accepting the traditional authorship, it is impossible to identify the occasion. Nor is it necessary. No choice is demanded between the historical and predictive interpretations. They fuse, and in their fusing reveal how prophecy is inspired. Some awful experience of pain, bodily and mental, had befallen David. As his habit was, he sought relief from the unbearable agony in poetry. As poets do in the rush and surge of their effort to communicate their emotion, the psalmist clutched at imagery from every corner of his experience. He had seen the fierce bulls of the plains beyond the Golan Heights clustered to attack. He had heard of or seen the sadistic tortures invented by the cruel folk of Tyre and the Phoenician coast, the nailing of a living man by hands and feet . . . and in the wild search for any words, any image of horror and desperation by which to give body and expression to his extremity of pain, David caught at such pictures of evil and flung them desperately into verse. But mark this, for here lies the awesome truth. So utterly complete was his committal of that which tortured him to God that the temporal merged with the eternal, the human with the divine, and the theme broke the boundaries of the present and touched that which was yet to be. This cannot be other than a preview of the Crucifixion, a passionate and fearful picture of Calvary. It was so seen by the Crucified Himself and accepted as the expression of His own desolation. It seems to be the way with God, that He takes a shred of surrendered experience, a mite cast in the treasury, a few fish and some bread, and, with magnifying and infinitely creative touch, transforms them. David provided at immense cost the raw material of a day of misery, persecution, rejection and defeat, and God, accepting the gift, conferred immortality upon it. So prophecy is made. The sufferer broke from time and place into the other dimension of being where God dwells. His mortal words became immortal.

**Commentary**

**1–5** There is desolation in the darkness, the blackness of God's seeming silence and withdrawal, rendered more dreadful by the knowledge that God is holy and abhors the evil which encompasses the sufferer, and more poignant by the long experience of the good of all the past that prayer was once answered, vindication once sure.

**6–8** There is no light in the darkened sky above. The victim dares to look around and there is no escaping the scene at Calvary, even to the scorn of the priests who had come in their last and deepest degradation to taunt the man who hung in agony. There was a terrible occasion on which Christ spoke of a sin beyond the reach of pardon. That sin can only be found in those who, in their last surrender to evil, pass a point of no return. This last damnation of the soul can precede, if a man so wills it, the death of the body. There are signs and tokens of such final sinning. One was seen at Calvary when the murderers of Christ publicly jeered at His last desolation. Verse 8 echoes the whole scene as Peter described it to Mark (15.29–34).

**9–11** All faith seemed betrayed, the long conviction and certainty which had led to the confrontation with evil. Christ was tempted in all the ways in which the race He came to save know temptation. Inexplicable though it may be, this statement must mean that Christ knew the dark hours of the soul when the mind faces the bleak thought that all which had upheld courage and had made the very pattern of a godly life, appears a lamentable mistake, a mockery and a delusion. The tormented one seems in agonized despair to traverse what had seemed so certain, so sustaining. Could it all be wrong?

**12–18** And if so were these right? Had they, this leering, evil mob, chosen the better part? They crowded round to gloat, destroy, enjoy the spectacle of unutterable pain. The scene is again the dimmed and blooded view from the cross. Can it be other than this? The theme truly breaks out of its century and strides a thousand years with vs. 16 and 18. The centuries blend and blur and we glimpse an edge of the meaning of the strange phrase about one 'slain from the foundation of the world' (Rev. 13.8, KJV). And seek to grasp one further thought. 'God was in Christ . . .' God suffered here. The Trinity was not divided into a Father chastising the Son, and a Son enduring chastisement, His heart, as a hymn has it, 'a sheath' for Jehovah's 'flaming sword'. The pain of the cross quivered through the universe.

**19–21** These verses form a transition from the agonized cries and despair of the first half of the psalm to the triumph of the end. If the psalm symbolically covers the whole span of time from Calvary to the Empty Tomb, the moment of triumph may be fixed in v. 21 where De Witt only of all translators has the courage to follow the Hebrew rather than ancient versions and to punctuate with what must surely be the proper distribution of the sense: '. . . and from the horns of the wild cattle – THOU HAST ANSWERED ME!' The tense of the verb becomes historical perfect. Peril and horror reach a climax: 'Save me from the lion's mouth, yes, from the horns of the wild oxen . . . You have answered me.' From the abandonment and desolation with which the psalm began, the sufferer passes to consciousness of deliverance. Is this the moment of resurrection in the wider prophetic meaning of the psalm?

**22–26** Leupold remarks that 'there is even a formal difference between the first half of the psalm and the second.' In the first half the statements of the individual verses are shorter, like gasps breathed in distress. Now they are longer, for the speaker is delivered and free from pain. In the more immediate experience of the psalmist, the transformation may represent a fact of remarkable deliverance. Indeed from the glad cry: 'You have answered me', there may be a second tract of writing, separated from the first by the events which brought deliverance. Verses 25 and 26 may represent a feast of celebration, given in pursuance of a vow. Lev. 7.16 seems to suggest such a social testimony.

**27–31** In mystic language the meditation expands and has its major significance for us in a messianic expectation. Verse 29 seems to refer to the ultimate triumph of Christ: 'Yea, to him shall all the proud of the earth bow down; before him shall bow all who go down to the dust, and he who cannot keep himself alive.' 'Posterity shall serve him,' the next verse continues; 'men shall tell of the Lord to the coming generation . . .' Such a consummation still tarries, but has the tormented world any other hope?

### Conclusion

Paul has a mysterious phrase about 'making up' or 'completing' the sum of Christ's sufferings (Col. 1.24) as though it could be a Christian's solemn privilege to be one with Christ in the pain of the cross. If we accept the dual meaning of this psalm the writer passed through some such experience in prospect rather than in retrospect. With such passionate completeness was his pain surrendered that it was absorbed into the heart of God.

## Read Psalm 23; 2 Samuel 17.27–18.4

### Occasion and author

If the preceding psalm was difficult to relate to one specific event in the life of the writer, the Shepherd Psalm is simple. We left the fugitive David at Psa. 6 struggling out of the dark Jabbok Gorge to the upland sheep country round Mahanaim on whose loyal people he was retreating. Mahanaim lay near Jabbok on the northern bank, a pleasant place of which George Adam Smith, Palestine's famous geographer, wrote in his great book with lyrical enthusiasm. There were, when Smith wrote at the end of the last century, pasturelands, irrigated orchards, crops, brakes of oleanders and tillage. In that unchanging countryside it is likely to have been somewhat the same in David's day. Mahanaim was a staging post of caravans on the inner curve of the Fertile Crescent, 'a fine strong town', said Josephus, and an ideal rallying point for the royal forces. David's anxieties were speedily suppressed. He was received with enthusiasm by the alien Shobi, by Machir, a local sheikh who had once supported Saul, and by the rich rancher, the magnificent old Barzillai, who placed all he had at the disposal of his king. The weary group was entertained with oriental courtesy, perhaps as the sun sloped on the first carefree afternoon David had had since the grim retreat to Jordan began.

The wealthy shepherd was host, and this guess at the historical background solves for ever the excruciating attempts of unimaginative commentators to divide the finest of all ancient lyrics into two poems.

Picture the royal minstrel rising at the banquet's end to thank his shepherd host and touching the strings. For the first time the ears of men receive the moving simple phrases of the most famous of all the psalms. And what a compliment to Barzillai. The unknown translator of the King James Version caught the simplicity of it all to perfection. It is a good translation, free from error, and should be exempt from all heavy-handed revision. The cadences are fragile and are easily broken.

**Commentary**

**1** The shepherd image pervades Scripture. Moses, destined to lead a people to nationhood, was sent to learn his task by the shepherding of sheep. The Lord claimed the image for Himself, and it captivated early Christian art as the graffiti of the Catacombs demonstrate. It fills the Asaph psalms, as a look at the sequence of the psalms' eighth decade will show (74.1; 77.20; 78.52,70,71; 79.13; 80.1).

**2** In the East the shepherd went before. He knew his sheep, and was known by them. Flocks could mingle and separate out again at the familiar call. Pasture was scarce, and the shepherd would lead his small flock from place to place, making sure that, at the proper time, water would be found, and the weary animals could find rest and shade when the sun stood high and the day was hot. And note that this psalm appears to begin at high noon. The morning wandering is pictured as already over, and the time of rest and refreshing is at hand. How curiously this fits the conjectured circumstances. The royal guests, already weary with a morning's march, during which the leader was perhaps hard put to it to shake off the dark forebodings of the night, emerged from the vale of the Jabbok as the heat of middle-day was mounting. 'Green pastures' and 'still waters' were their welcome, both in the realities of the Gilead landscape and the warmth of their friends. They were ready for both.

**3** The theme rises in v. 3. It is a harassed man, still shrinking from the horrors of the night just done, whose soul is 'restored', no dumb sheep. And 'paths of righteousness' are for human walking. So He guides 'for his name's sake'. In Hebrew thought a name was never remote from the character and the personality, and this beautiful phrase means, in consequence, 'because he is what he is' – a true shepherd. In the very nature of God lies our confidence.

And we should note, whenever we seek God's guidance, that He can never lead in other than 'the paths of righteousness'.

**4** If the placing of the psalm is correct, the 'valley of the shadow of death' was a memory of the night before, the black night, the confining cliffs, both the very symbols of the spirit's dark hour. There are some few quibbles over the translation of *tsalmaveth,* but the common version is close enough, and has established a phrase in the English language. Darkness is almost an instinctive symbol of the horrible, the uncanny and the evil in all literature.

Such total darkness was the burden of Samson's lament as Milton pictures him in *Samson Agonistes*: 'eyeless in Gaza, at the mill with slaves':

*O dark, dark, dark amid the blaze of noon,*
*Irrecoverably dark, total Eclipse*
*Without all hope of day.*

And such quotation could be multiplied. It is to be noted, however, that in contexts of faith the psalmist's note of hope and courage is picked up. In the darkness is a Presence, and with that assurance those who trust walk firmly and with confidence. 'Moses went into the dark – *where God was*', and David, stripped now of the uncanny dread of the night's apprehensions, faces 'the valley of the shadow of death' with no fear of evil, for the Shepherd, armed and wise, is there.

Bunyan quite misses a point in his allegorical account of Christian walking through the Valley. He should somehow have introduced a Guide. As he has it the section on the Valley is the weakest part of his allegory.

C. S. Lewis is perhaps happier. He does not mention the Valley, but has it in mind in the climax of the Temptation in his exquisite *Perelandra*. He pictures the tense scene in the palpable darkness of the night and Ransom's utter loneliness and fear. . . . 'But while he was thinking thus, as suddenly and sharply as if the solid darkness about him had spoken with articulate voice, he knew that Maleldil was not absent. That sense – so very welcome yet never welcomed without the overcoming of a certain resistance – that sense of a presence which he had once or twice before experienced on Perelandra, returned to him. The darkness was packed quite full . . .'

Return to the sustained imagery of the poem. The 'rod' and the 'staff' are the shepherd's tools, the club and the crook. The club was a weapon, a stout stick with a ball of bitumen and metal studs, an arm against predators. The crook, ancestor of the curved walking-stick, was the age-old implement of those who shepherd sheep. It was an instrument of guidance, but above all of restraint, a symbol of wise control. The colossal figure of Rameses the Second in the entrance hall of the temple of Abu Simbel, so precariously lifted, at the world's insistence, above the waters of Aswan, show the Pharaoh with crossed arms, one hand holding a flail-like lash, with multiple thongs, the other a crook. The monarch threatened punishment. He also professed control. The crook spoke of his gentler constraint. It is an old royal claim. A prayer of the Sumerian king, Kudur-Mabug, discovered in an inscription at Ur, expresses the hope that he may ever serve as Nannar's 'dear shepherd'. Another petty monarch of the same river-valley, in the same exalted mood, called himself 'the shepherd of mankind'.

The crook, slipped round the sheep's neck, restrains. And how often does our rashness need restraint and our haste and misdirected zeal the checking strength of the Great Right Hand. We are wise to yield to that sense of restraint. C. S. Lewis in the magnificent analysis of temptation in *Perelandra* (*Voyage to Venus*) already quoted, speaks of a moment when 'the whole atmosphere seemed charged with disapproval', and a compulsion in the very air which forbade all tampering with truth . . . 'The falsehood which sprang to his mind died on his lips. In that air, even when truth seemed fatal, only truth would serve . . .'

Note, before leaving this rich image, the intruding pronoun: 'Thy club and thy crook, *they* comfort me'. The word is in the Hebrew text. *They* are there when all else fails, God's protection, God's restraint.

**5** The theme returns to the long table in Barzillai's farmhouse. To be sure, Absalom was still in Jerusalem. His scouts were out, and mobilizing every disaffected group in Israel to march against his father. It could be many weeks before a host conformable to the prince's megalomaniac ideas could be marshalled, marched through the difficult wilderness, and flung on the king's *élite* corps at Mahanaim. There was war in the air, however much a cool appraisal of the logistics might convince the king and Joab that an attack could not well be immediate. C. S. Lewis, quite uncharacteristically, misinterprets this verse. He ranks the verse, astonishingly, with some of the imprecatory passages which, again, he quite fails to set in a meaningful context. He writes: '. . . after the green pastures, the waters of comfort, the sure confidence in the valley of the shadow, we suddenly run across: "Thou shalt prepare a table for me against them that trouble me" – or, as Dr. Moffatt translates it, "Thou art my host, spreading a feast for me *while my enemies look on*." The poet's enjoyment of his present prosperity would not be complete unless those horrid Joneses (who used to look down their noses at him) were watching it all and hating it . . . the pettiness and the vulgarity of it, especially in such surroundings, are hard to endure.'

Lewis was, of course, misled by the two faulty translations which he quotes. The enemy were not, at the moment, a physical presence, or even an immediate danger. It was, however, a nagging and obsessive fact that David was not free from their presence for a single waking hour. Loyalists were flowing in; arms were being collected; the detachments were being trained for the type of terrain Joab had to use in Gilead, rugged oak woods and mountain slopes, cut with deep ravines . . . The breath of the foe was in the air, in the spies' reports, in rumour filtering down the wilderness tracks.

**6** Building confidence out of the lessons of the past as we shall see him do in the opening verses of Psa. 27, David feels that, delivered as he had been from the grim perils of the week behind him, nothing more could possibly befall. The 'house of the Lord' does not mean the Jerusalem temple. It had not yet been built. As one might expect, the phrase has been laid hold of by the unimaginative commentators as an excuse for their common obsession – to late-date Scripture. The phrase merely sustains the imagery. It is a glimpse as we have seen, more common in the Old Testament than is commonly recognized, of another life, a new dimension of fellowship beyond the grave. Calvin wrote: 'This sentence shows that he finds no complete satisfaction in the pleasures or blessings of earth, but sets himself a goal in heaven to which he relates everything.'

Calvin might have gone further. It is another facet of what we saw in the passionate verses of Psa. 22. We saw the writer snatching an image to express his agony from the foul sadism of Tyre, and breaking uncannily through to the vision of the crucified Christ, a millennium down the corridor of history.

So also in Psa. 23. David touched the heights of song, not this time in purging his soul of grief and wretchedness, but in giving voice to gratitude, relief and joy. In closing his song he broke some barrier and touched a higher truth than men were clearly to know until One who died, and passed through the valley of the shadow of death in the ultimate and final sense, made clear by His rising again that there was something else beyond the sunset and evening star.

**Conclusion**

Perhaps this psalm was David's last great utterance. Perhaps there was little time for song in the demanding days which lay ahead. As another was to remark: 'For everything there is a season: and a time for every matter under heaven . . . a time to rend and a time to sew, a time to keep silence and a time to speak' (Eccles. 3.1,7). It was a time now to work, to sew together the torn fragments of authority, a time to build. The Indian Summer of David's energy, which had found expression in a new burst of poetry, also revealed itself in his dynamic leadership, active and visible, until the sudden weakness which the shrewd Joab saw, when the commanders persuaded the old fighter not to take the field.

Back in Jerusalem, restored again to his shaken throne, there was a span of declining years, shot through with much sorrow. We shall meet the royal psalmist in many more psalms but it may be guessed that there were few outbursts of true poetry over the years ahead. He had said most of that which he was called upon to say. It was very vital truth.

The New Testament was to make explicit that which David, ahead of his century's understanding, grasped, that sin, abandoned and confessed, was forgiven, and not only forgiven but forgotten, with the forgiven sinner made whole and renewed by the touch of the forgiving Hand. It is thus that the poet-king of Israel draws close to us, assumes features familiar to our mind, stirs, like some tragic hero, our pity, and becomes, in the completeness of his surrender to God in the midst of fault and folly, our exemplar and our guide. There, too, stands our hope in God.

# 24

**Read Psalm 24; 2 Samuel 6.1–15; 1 Chronicles 16.1–37**

**Occasion and author**

The occasion of this hymn of triumph is a climax in the life of David. He had captured Jerusalem from the Jebusites to be his royal capital. The city sits high on the land's spine of hills, magnificently situated, and almost impregnable. The awful siege in Vespasian's and Titus's day, when the city defied for so long all the Empire's strength, demonstrated this. It was an ancient stronghold at whose gates (7, RSV) Abraham had met the great Melchizedek. It is significant that the psalms quoted in the Chronicler's account of the events (1 Chron. 16.1–37) take us back to Abraham. David sought now a final symbol. The Ark was a sign of God's presence, and it had lain at Kiriath-jearim for half a century. The first attempt to bring it home had ended in ill-omened failure, but now all was well, and with great pomp and gladness the procession of priests and Levites accompanied by the royal psalmist himself carried the beautiful piece of holy furniture up to the ancient gates of the city. Josephus says that there were seven choirs of singers and musicians, and if the choral chanting of the psalm was to cover the length of the procession, this tradition may well be true. No doubt the key questions of vs. 3, 8 and 10 were called aloud by a single voice, some Stentor among the officiants who was answered triumphantly with the burst of music and song which followed.

**Commentary**

**1** David was clearly anxious that neither Ark nor hill should be considered the dwelling-place of deity – some tribal god, confined, like any baal of the Canaanites, to a narrow house. The Ark was no more than symbol, with the law within, and the unearthly beings gazing down on an empty mercy seat. Hence the stress on the Lord's work as creator. The sequence of ideas is natural – God's universal sovereignty, passing to the righteousness He demands, and then, finally, to the events of the day. Inevitably, those who have approached the psalm with preconceived ideas find some compulsion to divide the poem into three, corresponding to three stages of evolution in the psalm's revelation of the 'Hebrew consciousness of deity'. David was mature enough in his view of God, and to begin with the psalm is to see in it only a natural sequence of ideas from which, and only from which, the concept of deity held by the author may be derived and understood.

**2** It is a similar heavy-footed approach which sees 'primitive Semitic cosmology' in the second verse. This is poetry and how natural to see the lands of earth rising from the vast oceans. Where these words are written on a summer's day in 1973, the Auckland isthmus where the New Zealand city lies between the Tasman Sea and the Pacific Ocean, interwoven and bound by the long tidal reaches of the eastern and western harbours, the ancient words of the psalm have exact and vivid illustration outside the window: 'He has founded it upon the seas, and established it upon the rivers' – or 'made it fast upon the streams . . .'

**3** Jerusalem on its crags rises ahead, and it is no light thing to claim citizenship of a community which David envisaged on this day of triumph. Who dare stand before such a God? cries the voice. Who can so claim to approach Him? 'Stand' implies a confidence like that of 1 John 2.28 which J. B. Phillips renders: 'So that, if he were suddenly to reveal himself we should know exactly where we stand, and should not have to shrink away from his presence.' The psalm seems to reach out to this consummation in Christ. 'Who shall stand?' Like some ritual challenge issued from a royal stronghold as visitors approach, the cry comes – and the ready answer.

**4** 'Clean hands and a pure heart' are the passport – in behaviour and in motive, in visible conduct and the character which forms it, these are the marks of the man who can face God. Good conduct can be the product of fear, and if fear is thus fruitful it is salutary. It was hunger that prompted the return of the Prodigal Son, and the father did not probe into the motives. But he is nobler who is reconciled to God in that inner sanctum of the being whence all conduct comes. The antiphonal exposition concentrates upon this thought. Such people do not 'lift up their soul' to what is false. They do not 'set their heart upon' the shams of life, those objects and aims which betray. Or, as the Jerusalem Bible puts it, their soul 'does not pay homage to worthless things', which, as an immediate corollary, lie, present a false face to the world, a pretence to society. Living is simpler without a divided mind. A curious word in Mark's Gospel tells of a fascination which John the Baptist had for Herod who murdered him. 'Herod revered John, knowing him to be a just and saintly man, and he kept him by him, and when he heard him was very perplexed, and yet he was glad to listen to him.' It was a curious dilemma, but a common one. Why was Herod perplexed? Because of a divided mind. He saw the right, but knew what it would cost. He saw with more clarity than some that he could not live in both camps, serve two masters, hold fast to his sin, but win salvation. He was perplexed because he could see no logical adjustment to his mode of life which would leave him the enjoyment of the vices he loved, and yet remove the load from his conscience.

His folly lay in the over-estimate of the worth of the trash he hesitated to abandon. No real or abiding pleasure is diminished by surrender to God. All else that matters or endures is given in Him. It is in the service of evil that things coveted are costly, and sham into the bad bargain. As Lowell puts it:

*At the devil's booth are all things sold,*
*Each ounce of dross costs its ounce of gold;*
*For a cap and bells our lives we pay,*

*Bubbles we buy with a whole soul's tasking.*
*'Tis heaven alone that is given away,*
*'Tis only God may be had for the asking . . .*

Herod, along with multitudes, found it difficult to see this simple truth.

**5,6** Such people as v. 5 describes 'receive . . . vindication' from the God of salvation; 'justification from the God of his deliverance' (as Smith and Goodspeed render). The theme almost breaks through to the New Testament doctrine of grace and imputed righteousness. At the end of v. 6, as though to allow such truth to soak into the soul, there is silence, as *Selah* indicates. The procession still moves on but all that is heard is the sound of moving feet. Great truth has been upon the lips, and the mind must apprehend it.

**7** But the gates of the old fortress of Zion are in view and dramatically the cry arises for their opening. 'Gates, raise your arches, rise, you ancient doors,' the Jerusalem Bible renders it, as though the very walls should open and the great wooden leaves swing back of their own accord before such a demonstration. God is coming in, throned in a multitude of hearts, as the glorious King.

**8** 'Who is He?' cries the single voice, dramatizing the watchman who demands name and password. The words and the answer are repeated. In the midst of the pageantry it must have been a thrilling moment, the procession perhaps pausing at the wall.

**9,10** The Lord of Hosts, 'the Commander of all of heaven's armies' (LB), is demanding admittance.

**Conclusion**

The psalm is best read in the context of its history. The Ark came to Jerusalem. In symbolism rich in its significance, the Lord was set in Zion. Others sought entry. Sennacherib beat upon the gates in vain. Nebuchadnezzar and Titus broke in and destroyed. So, if a mystic meditation is sought, with what Bunyan called the City of Mansoul . . . 'Behold,' said Christ, in another context, 'I stand at the door and knock . . .'

# 25

**Read Psalm 25**

## Occasion and author

Traditionally the psalm is ascribed to David, and the attitude taken here to tradition has been more than once made clear. Unless the challenge is serious, tradition should stand. On two grounds, neither of which can be taken seriously, the suggestion has been made that the psalm is post-exilic. It is, first, alphabetical, each verse beginning with a successive letter of the Hebrew alphabet – a mnemonic device. This, it is alleged, was not an early invention. It is difficult to see why an aid so obvious should not have been as old as the alphabet itself. Secondly, there is a mingling of 'wisdom literature', sententiously expressed truths, general statements of truth, which it is again alleged without foundation, did not find literary expression in the days of David.

It is possible that this group of psalms dates from a period of soul searching which David experienced after the days of challenge and triumph which followed the establishment of the Ark in Zion – a guess, but the editors may have known, or sensitively assumed, such a situation. The writer is conscious of opposition (2), of the need for wisdom beyond his own (4), of past unworthiness (7), of inadequacy (11), of disloyalty around him (15) and manifold problems (17).

## Commentary

**1** Prayer involves a certain 'lifting of the soul', an orientation of the life. Hence the opening of the Lord's Prayer. Hence the closing of the eyes as though to exclude the things of earth. Hence a posture of devotion.

**2** Hence, too, an affirmation of faith, and that tug of doubt which such an affirmation seems so often to provoke. The suppliant's soul has been dragged back to earth and the spectacle of encircling foes. He has trusted, and it is part of his plea that trust, publicly acclaimed, shall not be made the theme of his enemies' jubilation. To be ashamed, in David's view, was part of the pain of unanswered prayer. Ezra (8.22,23) faced and conquered this fear.

**3** The petition becomes universal. He belongs to a mass, a multitude, of those who look to God for aid like petitioners in the royal audience room. Let the rebels, the wilful traitors, rather, be abashed, their fine-laid schemes in disgraceful ruin.

**4** How desperately man, with the wall of the future's darkness before him, needs guidance! This theme recurs in David's prayers. To know the will of

God and how it applies to personal circumstances is the final and most blessed security in life.

**5** A security indeed which makes the true follower of God a pupil in the school of truth, ready and willing to apply ultimate truth in all of life's contexts, perplexities, decisions. It is a schooling which never ends – 'for thee I wait all day long' – no passive waiting, but alert watching for the movement of God's hand. It is the faith of Rom. 8.26–28.

**6,7** The divine Instructor needs no reminder of His very nature, of those qualities which have always been, but it is of the nature of man in his anxious plea to speak thus, especially when he is about to speak of sin which God must surely remember. It is 'mercy all, immense and free', and David, in such moments of penitence, shows a perfect understanding of the grace which was to be in Christ.

**8–10** It is because of His nature, His love, which emerges under rich and varied names in verse after verse, that sinners can expect, not chastisement, but instruction and guidance. They need only, in fact, the gentleness, and willingness to learn, the patience which looks for reality, the realization of ignorance which is the first step to knowledge. In no sphere of human activity can anyone learn in any other way. The arrogant, the self-sufficient, the boldly sure, are unteachable. Humility must precede all. And this presupposes a desire to keep His commandments. Without such committal God can do nothing with a life.

**11** The prayer, prompted by the words just uttered, returns to sin. 'For thy name's sake', an echo from the Shepherd Psalm, means 'because you are what you are, in accordance with your very nature'.

**12,13** This gust of anguish over past failure gone, the suppliant returns repetitively to the thought which has preoccupied him, but with a new tone of confidence. Those who reverence God can expect to be guided. They can expect tranquillity, for they have dealt with the sins which disturb peace and the evils which erode all quietness and confidence.

**14** The friendship (RSV) of the Lord can only be for those that trust Him. No 'intimate communion' (R. K. Harrison's rendering) is possible in any relationship if part of the personality is walled off and held back.

**15** One must be alert for His will, not looking at the snares of treachery spread along the path, but to the One whose universal view sees a landscape wider than the path.

**16** He alone can help the 'lonely and afflicted' (RSV).

**17–19** He alone can deal with the maladies of heart and mind and circumstance. In one crowded rush of words the psalmist lists them. 'Relieve the troubles of my heart, and bring me out of my distresses. Consider my affliction and my trouble, and forgive all my sins.'

The emotions, the thoughts, tear the person apart. 'But, oh, my two troubles,' wrote A. E. Housman, who knew no such refuge . . .

*'they reave me of rest*
*The brains in my head and the heart in my breast.'*

**20,21** These verses sum up and conclude the prayer. He trusts, he is prepared steadfastly to abide God's good time. He appears to linger, but it is for our instruction, to tarry, but only that we may learn the deeper lessons of life.

**22** The final verse may be to adapt the personal prayer to public use. It may be a formula by which the royal psalmist concluded every prayer. It is a conclusion standing outside the alphabetic structure – and how relevant in the embattled little land today.

**Conclusion**

God will be true to Himself, He will forgive in mercy and pattern the surrendered life. This presupposes no perfection. The psalmist reveals again and again his lively consciousness of imperfection. To those who practise this humility, this awareness, He reveals His outworking plan. Confidence, as Rom. 5.3–5 has it, grows from experience. Moffatt is worth reading on this psalm. Let him conclude: 'Kind and upright is the Eternal, he teaches any who go astray, guiding humble souls aright, teaching humble souls his way' (8,9). 'Preserve me and deliver me; ah disappoint me not as I take shelter with thee' (20) . . . As the old evangelical hymn had it: 'He is not a disappointment.'

**Read Psalm 26; Proverbs 1.7–19**

**Occasion and author**

Frequenting the holy place where the Ark now stood (8), a memorial and a reminder of God's presence, David was led to deep self-examination. It had all been, one may suppose, a strong emotional experience for him, and touched the very depths of his life. The kingdom was at peace, but the king was a man of war enough to know that peace was fragile, and like the Romans building walls round Verulamium deep in Britain during the Indian Summer of the second-century Roman Peace, he knew that, however remote the frontiers might seem, there was no peace save in vigilance and the overwhelming strength and guidance of God. He had searched his life for unrealized wrong and could look up with a good conscience. It was a blessed time, which tragically passed, eroded by the stresses of power and the corruption of an Eastern court. Meanwhile it held, and this small prayer is a facet of those days of confidence and dependence.

The psalm has been dismissed by some commentators as an expression of self-righteousness, and the writer linked with the Pharisee who 'went up into the temple to pray'. This is to miss the meaning. The mood is one of wary heart-searching, and it ends in a plea for God's vindication. It contains a different mood from the penitential attitude of the preceding psalm, but moods vary and the soul of man is not always of one colour. The place in the Psalter may have been determined by verbal echoes, and similarities of petition (25.2, cf. 26.1; 25.22, cf. 26.11; 25.16, cf. 26.11; 25.21, cf. 26.11; 25.5. cf. 26.3).

**Commentary**

**1** David had no secure and certain seat. Nelson Glueck, the rabbi-archaeologist, regarded him as a usurper. There was a party loyal to Saul. His course required care, visible integrity. Absalom was to show how fragile was the king's popularity. Hence the plea for vindication, a longing which often rises to David's lips.

**2** He bares heart and mind, emotions and motives, to the searching eye of God, a salutary and subduing prayer to pray:

*So wash me Thou, without, within,*
*Purge me with fire if that must be*
*No matter how, if only sin*
*Die out in me . . .*

Suddenly to find such a prayer answered might be a painful experience. To pray thus, and that is what the psalmist is doing, is not the action of a self-righteous man.

**3** We saw such protestations of innocence in 17.3 and 18.20–24, and must remember that it was in Christ alone that man found the measure for his wrongdoing and unworthiness. This is the Old Testament, and deep though David's conception of iniquity was, it was a thousand years before, in the light of Calvary, the full reality of the damage man had suffered could be truly seen.

**4,5** Some assertions could, however, be consciously made. There is no reason to suppose that, in the organization of his court and entourage, David did not consciously seek to award false, hypocritical and evil men. The two verses claim no more than a deliberate policy to exclude the unworthy from the royal presence and the affairs of state.

**6,7** The verses seem to locate the prayer. The king is at worship, and these are the thoughts which pass through his mind as he stands in the presence of God. It was his royal privilege to have the choir sing the words, and their public proclamation served notice on all that such were the principles of his rule. Warning mingled thus with testimony.

**8–10** There is no self-righteousness here. The psalmist has committed his life to God. He claims now that, dissociated from evildoers in conduct, he should also be spared the judgement justly falling on the rebels.

**11** Observe again that a claim to integrity is directly linked with a plea for redemption and grace.

**12** Only thus can the stance be sure, and the 'level ground' of security be firm beneath his feet.

# 27

**Read Psalm 27; 1 Samuel 17.41–48**

**Occasion and author**

The occasion of this song of jubilant faith is some high moment of victory, one of those days when it is bliss to be alive. The time of writing must surely be in those rich months when faith was vindicated, the long wait in trust and confidence ended, and when David was at last, by God's hand and not his own, in the royal seat which had been promised him. Victory over Absalom was poisoned by grief, so this can hardly have been a psalm of Mahanaim or restoration. There is a strong sense of youth about it all. Surely here is a younger man singing, not a weary warrior with a withered victory in his hands.

**Commentary**

**1** Each word is rich. 'God is light,' said John long after David. Light is apprehended only in relation to that on which it shines – the face of Christ, for example, in Paul's famous phrase (2 Cor. 4.6). God is a light on the path (John 11.8–10); a light on the goal (Phil. 3.14). And God is salvation. Note the turn of phrase. He *is*, He not only gives, salvation. It is the thought of 1 Cor. 1.30. It is part of the concept of a living Lord, worked out in v. 5. The fugitive, claiming asylum in the royal tent, receives it, unworthy though he might be. The powerful presence is his canopy and shield.

God is the stronghold of the psalmist's life. Like some Acropolis, some Capitol, some walled and garrisoned Zion, some peak high above the defenceless town into which the menaced may escape, so is the Lord Most High.

**2** Menaced indeed, the psalmist has been. He knew the terror of the charging, enveloping foe. He could not forget one moment printed for ever on his mind – Goliath, the hoplite, panoplied and armed, collapsing with a clash of iron as the hard round stone shot up under the helmet's rim as he threw back his head to laugh. It was inept of the RSV to change 'to eat up my flesh'. It was a remembered echo of what the huge Philistine had bawled across the little valley plain as the two armies watched, ranged along the hillslopes. The verse should be left as the KJV has it. It loses meaning unless, like the next verse, it is a memory of earlier triumph.

**3** 'Each victory will help you, some other to win,' said the old Sankey hymn, and this was a habit of thought with David. In this verse he remembers the terrifying moment when he walked down alone, to face Goliath alone, by the little brook which wound through the valley bottom. He was so reft, so lonely, so grimly exposed. The thought overwhelmed him as, sling held behind his back with his left hand, and thongs gripped in his right hand, he walked towards the ranged lines of the whole Philistine army. It was as though he was marching single-handed on the whole multitude.

**4** Again perhaps a pointer to the time. The 'house of the Lord' has been prominent in this group of psalms. David is remembering battle after victory, a beleaguered past from a triumphant present. The Ark was home, and he was now in peace.

**5** The blessed place was like a tent of refuge – and more: in the fertile imagination of the writer the temple that was to be, which, perhaps, at this time, he still hoped to build, rose in his mind, a bright image of hope.

**6** On the rocky hill-top where the Jebusites had once held their stronghold, and the alien's threshing floor showed the bare stone, he could see the beautiful shrine yet to be. There was something familiar about such stony summits, as the agile mind of the poet sprang from image to image. It was like some high-lifted platform in the familiar wilderness, whence he had often looked down on the pursuing patrols of Saul, his head 'lifted up above his enemies round about', then on the far wadi floor, now on the frontiers, visible if he looked east to the edge of the Moab range against the sky. And in the act he turns to worship.

**7** And to prayer. 'Seeking the face of God', realizing His presence, is the first movement of prayer. The Lord's Prayer again is the pattern.

**8–10** Some unknown situation of sorrow may lie behind this verse, unless the KJV translates correctly and the abandonment by loved ones is hypothetical – 'can a woman's tender care . . .' as the hymn puts it. 'Even if my father and mother were to forsake me,' as R. K. Harrison renders it, 'the Lord would adopt me.' The RSV is not at its best in this psalm.

**11** There is a touch of pathos in the plea for 'a level path'. David's feet had known the sheep tracks and the defiles of the rugged Judean wilderness. They had grown weary on the climbing trail. He longs for a patch of peace, of easy road, 'a plain path', as the KJV puts it. The trail we follow is often rough enough and overgrown in life. They are fortunate in whose minds this prayer finds no echo.

**12** A common preoccupation of David as we have already seen . . . He hated slander and shrank from treachery. The brevity of the historical account omits much. It was no easy land that Jesse's son was called upon to rule.

**13** In this broken verse a rather brilliant turn of rhetoric puzzled the rabbis. The KJV reflects what David wrote, and remedies the absence of a main clause by supplying the words: 'I had fainted . . .' dutifully italicized. David wrote: ' . . . unless I had believed to see the goodness of the Lord in the land of the living'. It was a subordinate clause without a main clause, quite magnificent in its strength. Admittedly this is not the best attested ancient reading, but it is one of those rare contexts in which the Lower Criticism may be denied the last word. It seems that the truncated structure should be the true reading. Perhaps the rabbis with tidy ideas of grammar, speedily adjusted the sentence, and both the Septuagint and the Vulgate lamely reflect the adjustment. The sentence was an aposiopesis, as the Greek term has it – a 'silencing off'. The KJV is prepared to accept the construction at Exod. 32.32. The first edition (1611) thus: 'And yet if thou wilt forgive their sinne:' Later and modern editions change the colon to a dash and a semicolon – ;. Moses does not presume to tell God what to do, and suppresses the main clause.

David wrote an aposiopesis. Alexander Maclaren and Derek Kidner, a century apart, seem to be the only commentators to recognize the power of the sentence. Maclaren translates: 'If I had not believed to see the goodness of Jehovah in the land of the living –!' One could be even more simple. Say the words slowly, punctuated with pauses of wonderment: 'Unless . . . I had . . . believed to see the goodness of the Lord . . . in the land of the living –!' Not, that is, in a far-off heaven, but here, outworking in daily life, in a blessed plan of guidance – unless this were my faith, I dare not think or say what might have befallen. The main clause is left for each of us to fill in. 'Unless I had believed that God was in control, that good must, however black the moment, be triumphant, unless I held this confidence of outworking purpose, I would have despaired, lost my life in cynicism, sin . . . Unless I had believed in God at that vital moment, in the clutch of that temptation, in that context of surrounding evil . . . I might have irrevocably fallen, abandoned my task, cast away my faith . . .' How strong a verse!

**14** Therefore, says David, wait, wait, as life had taught him to do. Be patient, enduring, trusting. Be strong, for so to battle on with foemen leaning on your shield calls for all you have and are. Be brave. God knows you need courage. But wait, wait. God's blessings are the reward of faith. That is why they tarry. You are part of a wider pattern, and the synchronizing of all the parts demands time. Abraham hasted and became the father of Ishmael and centuries of conflict ensued. Blessings, too, come when the life of the believer is ready for them. Moses had to wait. God could not use the prince of Egypt. He had to wait for the shepherd of Midian to be born. And so it ever is. Wait for the Lord.

**Conclusion**

There is nothing to add to a psalm which so triumphantly concludes itself. This is one of those psalms which should be memorized. When the heart is weary and the mind battered by the ills of life, it is sometimes a relief to allow thought to flow in the prepared channels of words long known and sanctified. Yes . . . unless I had believed . . .

# 28

**Read Psalm 28**

**Occasion and author**
There is no doubt that this psalm reflects the mood of Psa. 26, and no need to challenge the traditional authorship. It is full of echoes of the last five psalms. The words and imagery are unquestionably similar.

**Commentary**
**1,2** A prelude, marked by the anxiety of the suppliant, opens the psalm. There is the whiff of doubt. Does God hear? If not, there is no difference for the believer. He is like the damned, like the feckless multitude streaming to oblivion. The suppliant lifts his hands, reaching symbolically for God, demonstrating their emptiness. The 'holy sanctuary' is where the Ark now stands – and the temple of David's fond dreams, a building of the mind.
**3,4** It is interesting to watch the psalmist's mind at work. The thought of the godless prompts the fear that the ultimate of evil fates would be inclusion in their disaster, to be swept away in the torrent of their sin. Let God set them apart, he begs, and judge them as their sins of hand and tongue demand. 'Drag me not away,' the opening words of v. 3 run. It echoes strongly Psa. 26.9. It is the verb of Job 24.22, which the Jerusalem Bible renders: 'But he who lays mighty hold on tyrants rises up to take away that life which seemed secure.' The image is the mighty hand of law, snatching a criminal from his imagined security to judgement.
**5–7** 'As in many psalms,' says Maclaren, 'the faith which prays passes at once into the faith which possesses.' Fear has vanished, perhaps after a pause between vs. 4 and 5. Praise and exultation invade the theme.
**8,9** Remembering that he is king of Israel, the suppliant widens the horizon of his prayer. His people invade his thoughts.

**Conclusion**
The psalm illustrates how a pattern of words, a liturgy fastened in the mind, can assume new meanings and gather new needs, new pleas, new situations into the structure of its words. Such an aid the Lord's Prayer can be to Christians. So can many a psalm.

# 29

**Read Psalm 29**

## Occasion and author

Storm and sunshine have stirred much poetry. David was a poet and can be allowed his creative moods. There is, say the archaeologists, a Ugaritic psalm on a similar theme, with Hadad, lord of storm, in place of God. Ovid has a poem on a storm at sea. Luke has a piece of fine prose. Shelley has some fine lines on storms in more than one poem. The phenomena of earth and sky are constant, and no literary genealogies are necessary. David, like Tennyson's Odysseus, had his band of stalwarts who 'ever with a frolic welcome took the thunder and the sunshine'. He saw from cave mouth and rock shelter the progress of many a thunder-front down the long rift in the land. He was in a mood to write, remembering 'emotion in tranquillity', Wordsworth's definition of poetry which we have already quoted, and so he put together this beautifully constructed poem.

## Commentary

**1,2** The Prelude. God is the Lord of Nature, and the power of a thunderstorm is a mighty manifestation of nature's power and the smallness of man. No superstition lurks in this any more than in the familiar verse quoted in the comment on Psa. 7.

**3,4** First Strophe. The storm is pictured coming in like Elijah's thunder heads, uplifted coils of cloud like a giant hand. The weather came in from the Mediterranean, burst against the Lebanon Range and swerved south, intensifying as it was caught and channelled in the vast trench of the Jordan Valley with its southward thrusting winds.

**5,6** Second Strophe. It is this movement of the rolling tempest which is caught in these two verses. The psalmist pictures the great mass of nimbus sweeping on to Lebanon. He knew all about the cedar forests which the Phoenicians worked, and which Solomon was one day to exploit. He pictures the seaward Lebanon Range and the long ridge of Hermon which closes the Beqaa behind it, blurred and dimmed in the pouring rain, losing all the quiet stillness they showed under the sunshine, till one could imagine that they, not the beating tempest, were moving. Note the repetitions artistically conveying the long, long roll of the crashing thunder. One phrase fails to convey the notion of continuity. Two phrases render it strikingly. Sirion, of course, is a Phoenician name for Hermon.

**7–9** Third Strophe. With down-stabbing lightning like the hewing strokes of some mighty axe, an image perhaps suggested by the assault on the Lebanon cedars, the storm goes past the watcher on the Judean uplands, to die away among the oaks of the Kadesh wilderness to the south. 'Flashes forth' (7) is translated by some 'hews out' ('hews out flames of fire' [Maclaren]), and the great axe is now at work on other trees. (Note RSV 'makes the oaks to whirl' (9), obtained by a different vocalization from that which gave KJV 'makes the hinds to calve'). Wind and lightning send the leaves snowing down, as they do if a shaft strikes down or near any tree.

**10,11** Postlude. God who, in the psalmist's mind had sat unmoved above the global tumult of the Flood, is still calm above the din of storm. The word for 'flood' is found elsewhere only in the Genesis account of the Deluge, and that must be the meaning here. Like the quietness on Galilee when Christ cried: 'Peace, be still', the uproar of nature dies with the exhausted tempest in the wilderness – and God remains.

**Conclusion**

So with life's storms:

*The wind it plies the saplings double,*
*It blows so hard 'twill soon be done . . .*

The tempests of the heart, the tumults of the world, roll by and pass. God remains. It is well, under the dark nimbus, to remember that above is the tranquil blue.

**Read Psalm 30; 1 Chronicles 21.18–26**

**Occasion and author**

The ancient heading seems to point to the dedication of the temple-site as the background for this hymn of consecration. The language fits, tradition in early societies was a much more strongly linked chain than can easily be imagined today, and the psalm, in accordance with its title, is grouped with others alluding to 'the house of the Lord', David's unfulfilled dream.

**Commentary**

**1** The writer has been 'drawn up', and the word suggests rescue from the horrifying imprisonment in a disused cistern such as Joseph endured (Gen. 37.23–28) and Jeremiah (38.6–13). The mysterious episode of the census, which seems to imply some emergence of royal pride on David's part, ended in the visitation of pestilence, always a fearful experience in ancient society, a terror made more acute by the glee certain to be felt beyond the pagan frontiers.

**2** David had fallen back on prayer. He had no other hope, a sombre fact to some who live in carelessness of God but find, in the straits of life, the old instinct rise in a cry for help beyond themselves.

**3** And prayer had found an answer. Amid a flood of death he had remained alive.

**4** It is difficult to envisage the choral circumstances. Perhaps it was a solo to this point of personal testimony. Then comes a sudden call for the whole choir or congregation to participate in the glad occasion. The Hebrew says: 'give praise to His holy remembrance' and the RSV renders 'His holy name'. His name, of course, contains the memory of all God was, and all God had done. The KJV need not have been altered.

**5** The beautiful second member of the KJV rendering has become an expression of hope dear to the English language. It falls short a trifle in losing the touch caught by Moffatt and Knox: 'tears may visit us at night . . .'; 'sorrow is but the guest of a night . . .'

**6** A confession lies here. 'Jeshurun waxed fat, and kicked . . . then he forsook the God who made him, and scoffed at the Rock of his salvation' (Deut. 32.15).

**7** Under the stress of trouble he saw the fragility of prosperity, and how utterly dependent upon God he was. 'I was dismayed,' he says. 'I was at peace no more,' Knox puts it.

**8** Such a loss of peace is salutary if it turns the stricken soul back to the Giver of all peace.

**9** A curious plea, which underlines the blessing the Christian holds in his confidence of another life. The Old Testament believer, as was stressed above, had more assurance of another life than some have been prepared to grant. Nevertheless there was no clear confidence, a faith which could become part of the experience of living. David here betrays this uncertainty. If praise is precious to God, he seems to say, then let Him retain His worshipper in life. Look at poor Hezekiah's prayer in Isa. 38.18, 19.

**10** The security, the prosperity of v. 6 are truly gone. Here is a desperate man appealing in utter simplicity.

**11** And here is the phenomenon we have noted before, which was either part of the experience of prayer or a literary device in the psalms to promote faith. It is better to regard it as both. The plea has broken through to confidence and faith lays hold of what was first the subject of agonized petition. Note that in the Chronicler's account (1 Chron. 21.16) it is stated that David and his court actually sat in sackcloth in the time of their disaster – a point which reinforces the contention that the psalm belongs to this occasion.

**12** The Hebrew says 'glory' – a word commonly used of God (e.g. Psa. 19.1). Used of man (e.g. Pss. 16.9; 57.8), it must mean the glorious part of man, the faculty discussed in the study of Psa. 8. Man is 'crowned with glory' because he has been entrusted with the solemn responsibility of choice. He knows God, but can reject Him. He knows good and evil, and can choose evil. He understands that life is more than bread, and can dedicate himself to bread. He can kill, in spiritual suicide, the better part of him. Or he can regard, as the psalmist appears to do in this bold metaphor, his 'glory' as all that matters, the heart (Knox), the soul (RSV), the real self. Man needs a vocal soul.

# 31

**Read Psalm 31; 1 Samuel 23.19–29**

## Occasion and author

The traditional heading ascribes the psalm to David and the personal agony which features in the prayer could well fit the period of David's escape into the desert of Maon and its strongholds. Maon, the modern Khirbet Ma'in, some eight miles south of Hebron, is open sheep country, and an invasion route from the Philistine lowlands. The manhunt of Saul was deflected by a Philistine raid.

On the strength of phrases which appear in Jeremiah, for example, 'fear on every side', which occurs six times in the prophet, together with a similarity of sentiment and language, some have suggested that Jeremiah wrote the psalm. The similarity of language could mean nothing more than that the psalm was a favourite with the trouble-ridden prophet. He was not the only sufferer who found sustenance for his spirit in the words of old pain, aspiration and devotion, which fill the Psalter.

## Commentary

**1–8** The psalm falls logically into three divisions of which these verses form the first. They form a developed theme not uncommon in the psalms, but there is no need to postulate some process of conflation to account for it. To be sure, there is the progression from the heart-cry of pain and need to the quietness and confidence in answered prayer noted several times before, but rounded sequences of such a sort are to be seen in Christian hymns.

The plea not to be 'put to shame' (1) is not infrequent. The worshipper commits not only himself but his God, before a watching world, and feels, as most Christians have at some time felt, that God's name as well as their faith are put somehow publicly to the test. It is no mean thing, as Elijah put it, to be 'very jealous for the Lord'. The imagery of the psalmist's confidence is full of the rugged rock citadels of the Judean wilderness, those Masadas of the ravines and hills which had more than once stood the fugitive in good stead.

Verse 5 stands sanctified by the Lord's own use of it (Luke 23.46). During those last days of His Passion He lived much in the Old Testament and the Psalms. Observe that committal of the life is followed in the second member of the verse by the cry of confidence. From this point on to the end of the section the wave of faith flows on.

**9–13** The movement from dejection to confidence is repeated. It is as though the glad grasp of God's reality which filled the last four verses had slipped, and the suppliant finds relapse into pain and wretchedness. Surely this is not an unknown experience, and it is a prosaic approach to demand of such a poem an ordered movement from conflict to victory. Perhaps the psalm was the record of a night's wrestling with pause and resumption in the writing. The first two verses show the writer back in despondency, but v. 10, which speaks of iniquity (KJV), probably needs amendment. Most versions follow the Septuagint, which omits one letter from the Hebrew word and reads 'misery' (literally 'beggary' or 'humiliation'). It might be difficult to justify the reading of the Septuagint, and it is not uncommon in the midst of earnest prayer to be suddenly and abasingly confronted with personal unworthiness. The matter of what the psalmist wrote may therefore be left in doubt, but with a strong presumption in favour of the traditional reading. Into this live consciousness of inadequacy, comes the old fear of shame before a hostile world. In superstitious fear his associates shun him. The misfortunes, so obviously loaded on the sufferer's head in the Old Testament context, suggest to the shallow and the timid some overshadowing cloud of divine disapproval, which can cast its shadow on those nearby. Friends drop off. The time-serving crowd see no advantage in further fellowship with the visibly God-forsaken. The next step is active hostility replacing passive disloyalty, and abandonment is complete. It all becomes a dark and hostile world, a ring of besieging terror, closing, closing in whispers urgent in the dark. The depths of abandonment are touched. It is the dark night of the soul.

**14–18** Trust gains the upper hand in this Apollyon conflict. An affirmation sums it up, 'My times are in thy hand'. It is a case of 'every step, every mile of the way'. What are our 'times'? The Hebrew word is the one used in the famous passage of Ecclesiastes (3.1–8): 'a time to be born, a time to die . . .' and the rest. One might have expected the translators of the Septuagint to have used one of the two Greek words for time, which means the opportune, the fit and the proper time (*kairos*). Instead they use *kleroi,* which means 'lots' and seems to inject incongruously a notion of chance into the phrase. The psalmist's whole confidence is that there is no accident. God controls events and experiences, overrules, permits, and out of all committed circumstances extracts good and blessing. 'Every man's life,' Maclaren comments, 'is a series of crises, in each of which there is some special work to be done or lesson to be learned, some particular virtue to be cultivated or sacrifice made. The opportunity does not return.' And the exciting feature for the Christian is that he does not know what hour, what event, what encounter, what word, what fragment, of a day's experience, may be of eternal significance. It behoves him to be where his 'times' are, in God's hand, ready at any moment to be used. There is something deeply moving in such expectancy.

The psalmist needs such confidence amid the surrounding clutter of arrogance, disloyalty and falsehood. The 'shining of God's face' is his desire. Let your presence radiate around your servant,' as Harrison puts it.

**19–22** The 'secret of his presence' (KJV) is the safe refuge which the knowledge of His encompassing grace affords. In such quietness and trust the old fears seem quenched. Steadied and stilled the panic of the earlier hour seems absurd.
**23,24** And thus steadied and stilled he can turn and bid others join him in the fortress and stronghold of his God. He remembers the word to Joshua; 'Be strong and of good courage' (1.6,7). The faithful may be called upon to wait, but such patience proves them faithful.

**Conclusion**
This is a psalm worth learning by heart. It is full of quotable phrases, like the Epistle to the Hebrews. It is perhaps more frequently quoted – in the New Testament, in Christian hymns, in prayer – than most other psalms. To hold it, woven with the thought, would be blessedness.

**Read Psalm 32; 2 Samuel 12.1–13**

**Occasion and author**
Accepting, as we have so far found good reason to do, the traditional authorship of the psalm, it remains to ask to what circumstances in David's life such an utterance may be ascribed. Conjecture need not stray far. The confession and poem in which the confession is embedded surely belong to the period of Psa. 51, and the agony of repentance which followed brave Nathan's denunciation of David's dire sin. It should, one might imagine, be placed after Psa. 51, because it reflects a somewhat quieter and reminiscent mood than that utterance of almost unbearable pain. Why the editor placed it at this point in the Psalter is difficult to say, unless it was in furtherance of an arbitrary desire to distribute the seven so called 'penitential psalms' throughout the whole collection. It seems hardly worth mentioning that there are critics who, following the endemic passion for late-dating which marks their school, have insisted that the psalm should be placed later than 500 B.C. on no other grounds than that it contains fragments common in 'wisdom literature' (e.g. vs. 8–11). The obtuseness of such criticism is amazing and would not be for a moment tolerated in areas of literature other than biblical.

This psalm meant much to Augustine, and Augustine's words: 'The beginning of wisdom is to know yourself a sinner', might form its caption. He had the words inscribed on the wall over against his bed, so that, when too ill to read, he might still be aware of their comfort. The theme was crystallized in a striking proverb (Prov. 28.13). Paul caught it up and developed it in Rom. 4.7. John, in one of the last utterances of the Bible, put it into the simplest of words (1 John 1.8,9).

**Commentary**

**1,2** In these two rich Beatitudes there are three words for sin, and three words for sin's forgiveness. The words, as most words do, contain embedded metaphors, and there is no need to pursue them to their literal origins. The totality of the meaning is what matters, and the theme implies that any human being ('he whose . . .'; 'the man to whom . . .'), whatever the form and fashion of his wrongdoing, call it what you will, can and will be forgiven.

**3** The folly is not to claim such grace by complete confession. There must be 'no deceit', 'no guile' (KJV), no words on the lips which do not gush from a repentant heart. But, given that, God cleanses. This verse is an insight into the silent months after David's murder and adultery, in which David appeared insensitive and beyond realization of the enormity of his sin. The land knew of it, and the hostile people murmured their resentment and their discontent. The court and its king had become encrusted and immobilized in the attitudes and aloofness of oriental monarchy. The leader no longer led. He posed as something more than man. He usurped arbitrary rights, and failed to realize the fragility of such hypocrisy. Nathan's courageous word shattered the shell and the man emerged. And if v. 3 is read aright, it appears that through the months of apparent disdain and unconcern there was misery of mind and heart which made his very body sick.

**4** The pressure of God's hand lay upon him, a weight like the heat of the burning summer sun. There is no peace, as Francis Thompson put it in *The Hound of Heaven*, for those whom God pursues, only panting flight. There is no rest when the Almighty Hand bears down upon the head, only aridity of heart and exhaustion. There is one escape, ever open, ever ready – surrender and confession.

**5** Verse 5 contains the blessedness of this moment. It is a simple act, and immediate in its effectiveness. Hence the interweaving in these words of confession and relief. 'At a bound,' says Maclaren, 'the soul passes from dreary remorse. The break with the former self is complete, and effected at one wrench. Some things are best done by degrees; and some, of which the forsaking of sin is one, are best done quickly.' C. S. Lewis sets that thought in his perceptive parable of the red lizard in his *Great Divorce*. More directly, it is the mirror-image of Nathan's words in 2 Sam. 12.13.

**6,7** Confession changes here to reflection, and no complicated theory of editing, conflation or anything else, need be invented to account either for this or the next change of attitude or mood in the closing four verses. The author need not have written his psalm in one passionate burst of inspiration, such as is apparent in, for example, Pss. 22 and 23. The pen could have been laid aside and the theme resumed. The purely personal experience could have been thoughtfully universalized. This psalm is, after all, called a 'maschil' or psalm of instruction, and that is what it becomes as the theme develops. In these verses the imagery of the wilderness, its sudden flash floods, its rocky strongholds, never far from David's mind, intrudes with some magnificence.

**8,9** The eye of God was a common thought. There is a word which implies 'in front of' which contains the notion. It is used, for example, in Judg. 18.6: 'Go in peace. The journey on which you go is under the eye of (in front of) the Lord.' The supreme illustration is the breaking of Peter (Luke 22.61) at a mere glance of the Lord. The concept is that God sees, watches, and although we appear to be alone, we are never out of sight. And being thus in view, love follows, and the impulse which knows no space or separation, directs aright. Only let the mind be sensitive and attuned to catch the hint, the message. This blessed awareness is that which sets us apart from the beast (9), the horse which needs the bridle, the mule, proverbial for dumb obstinacy.

**10,11** The psalm provides its own conclusion. In Psa. 51 David hopes that restoration will be so complete that he will teach others who sin the ways of God (13) and bring sinners like himself to the blessedness of his own experience. Here he visibly seeks to do so. The bold splendour of the imagery is sustained to the end, with the fine picture of God's mercy, round the forgiven and repentant man like a fortress wall.

**Conclusion**

This is one of the great psalms. Generally it is best to pass by dull and insensitive comment, but the salutary rule may be broken here. One commentator remarks that this psalm does not reach the higher levels of the Psalter since it reflects the common opinion held throughout the ancient Near East with reference to 'the relation of all sickness to sin'. It would be difficult to find a more gross misreading of the psalmist's description of his pain. It has the touch of Psa. 22 about it – the racked and dessicated body is the vehicle and expression of the mind's pain. And furthermore, is it not a fact that the pathology of body and of mind are intricately and damagingly commingled?

# 33

**Read Psalm 33; Isaiah 44**

**Occasion and author**

There is no clue to the authorship of this splendid hymn, nor can a guess be made about the occasion of its composition. Some suggest it was a paean of praise after the defeat of Sennacherib's invasion, and the mood might fit the hour. Others ascribe it to the brave days of the Maccabees. It could equally be Davidic. Speculation can go no further.

It occupies its anonymous position in the Psalter because it is in line both in spirit and composition with preceding psalms, and the rabbinical editors, sensitive to word and phrase, saw a point of contact between the end of the preceding psalm and the opening words of this. Observe also such echoes as Pss. 32.11 and 33.3, 32.10 and 33.22. The order of psalms in the collection sometimes had no more justification than this.

**Commentary**

**1–3** The verses suggest some maturity of practice in religious music. Praise in song as these verses conceive it is jubilant and commanding. The 'new song' is not that of a new age, and a new apprehension of God's ways with man (Rev. 14.3), but a new devotion infusing old words, a vibrant novelty springing from hearts newly moved by some moving event.

**4–9** A new discovery of God's faithfulness (4), a fresh insight into unchanging love (5) has driven the writer of the song to deeper wonder of a Creator (6), an awesome power behind all nature (7), who yet can communicate with the creatures of His making (8) and will bend strength so unimaginable to their good (9). The mood is that of Psa. 8.

Set the psalm, whenever it was written, in the context of ancient history. It is not often that the surviving fragments of the hymnology of those days is found to dwell on righteousness, justice and steadfast love (5). And compare the picture of effortless creation (7) with the absurdities of the Babylonian creation myth. As Paul maintained (Rom. 1.18ff.), the very spectacle of the universe should turn any contemplative mind to the discovery and worship of the Mind behind all matter.

**10–12** This is the theme of Isaiah's later musings. Look through Isa. 40 to 44, five noble chapters which set an eternal plan (11) over against the wild strivings of men to outwork a godless destiny. Psa. 2 raised the thought in brief. Unless ultimate justice prevails, unless God has a plan which finally will be demonstrated in its perfection, unless the rebellion which is called sin in the end falls by its futility, all faith is vain. The lesson of any life which commits itself to God shows the truth of these words, for the plan of God's will works out on the mighty stage of history, too wide-flung for any single eye to see, and also, in comprehensible microcosm in any individual life. The people 'chosen as his heritage' (12) understand. Verses 10 and 11 are the only suggestions of a specific historical occasion in the actual text of the psalm, but the choice remains wide.

**13–17** Swept by the tides of human strife as Palestine was, it was natural that men should wonder whether there was any divine concern for it all. The steadfast faith of Isaiah faced with the Assyrian invasion, and Jeremiah in agony over Babylon, was that God was never swept from His control. That which He permitted had a moral purpose and subserved some mighty end. The world is no different. The moral law still stands. Ruin still follows rebellion. Evil can provide no foundation save for evil. Good is never fruitless. Man plots, plans, and by his evil seeks to win his ends but, from the psalmist's day to this embattled century, it has never been demonstrable from history that, as Voltaire put it, God sides with the big battalions.

**18–22** Unimaginative comment of the sort which wearies the mind sees a 'liturgical addition' in these closing verses. There is no justification for such prosaic exposition. The psalm, for any sensitive reader, ends like many a Greek poem and oration on a quiet minor note, and yet a note personal, penetrating and summing up, in simplicity of phrase and teaching, the whole lesson of the psalm.

**Conclusion**

And that lesson surely is that the mighty God cares, too, for small things (18). The one who trusts is never out of sight. Patience (20), trust (21), hope (22), lie behind His shield (20). This, the Christian, with so much deeper understanding, is taught to hold and to believe.

# 34

**Read Psalm 34; 1 Samuel 21.10–15; 1 Peter 3.1–12**

**Occasion and author**

There is no reason to reject the ancient heading. David looked back upon his grave peril in the court of Achish as one of the disgraceful episodes of his life. Under the long stress of his life in the desert, a hunted refugee, his nerve had broken, and he had endured the dire temptations of treason. He had played with the dark idea of employing his rebel band against his own people. It was a day of shaken and diminished faith, and who can boast freedom from such undulations? Perhaps, too, he was in a trough of depression, and they are fortunate indeed who are spared the more sombre hours of the soul's experience. David sought the Philistines' court. Abimelech, like Pharaoh, was probably a dynastic name. The king received him with undisguised suspicion, as well he might, and David was reduced to feigning madness, a condition which, in many ancient contexts, earned a measure of immunity. Insanity could mean the dangerous indwelling of a god. In later moments of tranquillity David remembered his base subterfuge with shame and this song was his offering of repentance. It is built as an acrostic, the initial words largely following the alphabet, and so betokens no hasty or contemporary composition. It is a testimony penned long afterwards, a salutary exercise of recollection. 'Emotion recollected in tranquillity', in Wordsworth's phrase already quoted, could not be channelled to better purpose. 'Poetry,' says the same paragraph, 'is the spontaneous overflow of powerful emotions.' Those emotions can be painful.

**Commentary**

**1–3** Perhaps the psalm is located here because of the specific example it provides of the closing statements of the preceding hymn. To look back and to contemplate the peril from which God has delivered, is to be stirred to gratitude. Gratitude hardly differs from praise (1). Others, likewise brought low, the multitude who have in similar circumstances known the depths of humilation (2), will join in the jubilation that it is precisely at that point that God can most effectively act. From the proud He cannot but withdraw. Often, before He can bless, a man must be reduced to the depths. From that point only can he begin to climb.

**4–6** Such was the royal testimony. He had known the agony of shame and self-abasement before men. He could see the proud face of Achish as he dismissed him, half in wonder, half in scorn. He could see the puzzled faces of his men, aghast to see their dashing leader brought to such humiliation. Through the darkness of that day one light beamed. David reached for God (4). Before such a throne no suppliant need feel the sting of shame (5). A 'poor man' he was, every human resource stripped away (6). At that point God could move in to enrich.

**7–10** God had not abandoned him, as he had imagined, discouraged and sick in mind and soul, when he took a desperate remedy and soiled his reputation by retreat to Philistia. In v. 10 the Septuagint reads 'rich' for 'young lions' – the sense is better and the Greek version may hold the best tradition.

**11–14** David saw, as he always saw, value in lessons painfully learned. In the midst of the enormous distress of Psa. 51 he looks forward to a moment when again he could 'teach sinners God's ways' (51.13,14). In two or three rapid touches he lists the faults which had led to his folly. He had lacked the quiet reverence for an overruling wisdom which had so often sanctified his exile (11). He had turned to base deception (13). He had, in a word, confronted by the eternal choice, turned to evil (14). The passage is in the style of the opening chapters of Proverbs, no argument on any sound ground of literary criticism for its late dating, but rather a demonstration of the ethical teaching which marked the day. They were part of the heritage of Israel, as Peter shows (1 Pet. 3.10–12).

**15–22** The old indomitable confidence that God would, in the end, vindicate and save, emerges again. Ultimately, good must be victorious – the climax to which the whole Bible moves in the Apocalypse. To grasp that triumph, it often happens that the faithful must stare hopeless defeat in the face. They did this on Calvary. They must face an utter breaking (18). Then God can act. Evil may appear to flaunt its victory. But wait and see – and this is a lesson which many an older and mature Christian has learned and illustrated from personal experience.

## Conclusion

There is no better way of leaching a bitter and damaging experience from the mind than doing with it as David did in this psalm. He committed it to God and turned it into poetry. He used an evil thing for good, and it is the commonest experience of life, if life is lived in the patterns of God's will, to find pain, suffering, even sin itself, taken by the Creative Hand and transformed into something beneficent and good. David's shameful and disgusting pose at Achish's door has given the literature of faith such words as those in vs. 8, 14, 18 . . .

# 35

**Read Psalm 35; Mark 15.20–31**

## Occasion and author

There is little reason to doubt the ancient ascription of the song to David. It is an utterance of trouble and rejection and as such belongs to the days of exile or to the Absalom rebellion. The mood of protest and desperation over the mendacity and the treachery of men is found in other psalms, and this long and eloquent utterance might have had a place among them. The editor had many guiding principles. In this psalm there are enough verbal echoes of its predecessor for some motive to be found for so placing it. The editor, too, had some care for his readers' comfort, and mingled with his other principles of order a desire not to burden too heavily any one portion of the Psalter with an unrelieved load of pain and distress.

## Commentary

**1–10** The imagery is drawn from the experiences of guerrilla war. Holding some Thermopylae in a narrow pass against the vanguard of pursuit, David must more than once have heard the thud of feet beside him, the rasp of a drawn sword, the clink of an uplifted shield, and felt the joy of one to stand on right and left and keep the pass. 'I,' murmurs a voice beside him in the narrow path of trouble, 'am here to help' (3). The image of such a battle passes on to the rout of the pursuing foe. The counter-attack comes down the dry wadi as the band regroups. Like chaff from some threshing floor in a gust of the sirocco, they go down the path their attack has so confidently trodden. Darkness is falling. The very terrain fights against the foe, 'dark and slippery', and in the panic-filled gloom they imagine strong pursuit behind them. They sought to trap their victim. The desert betrays them and becomes, in fortune's grim reversal, the trap they had sought to contrive. It was just retribution (7) for they had sought to harm the innocent, and with swifter judgement than wronged man often sees, God had struck back and mightily delivered. The fact is humbly acknowledged (10). 'Bones', as in Psa. 51.8, suggests the whole man. The psalmist's whole being tingles with gratitude and praise.

**11–18** A second section follows, for the psalm is quite carefully constructed, in which the suppliant returns over the field of his pain. The sequence of thought is natural enough. With deliverance won, the mind has time to think of the experiences which led to the assault. David often expresses his loathing of treachery. Two further psalms (41 and 55) also linger on the theme. Christ suffered, indeed died, the victim of false witnesses, and the Jews had no monopoly of that base vice. There could hardly be words more loaded with sadness than 'my soul is forlorn' (12). The vicious treatment was the harder to bear when the psalmist remembered his own care, generosity and love towards those who now so grievously betrayed him (13,14). And now the same faces, in the imagery of the poem, seem to leer in a ring round one wounded and fallen in the street (15,16). It was the scene stoned Stephen saw (Acts 7.54) – or Christ crucified. The section ends, as did the first section of the psalm, with a turning in faith to God. Some have placed v. 18 elsewhere. It is obviously correct where it is.

**19–28** The cry which fills these verses is for vindication. The Christian who is the beneficiary of his Lord ('grace and truth came through Jesus Christ' – John 1.18) may not as appropriately pray with such vigour. At the same time, it is natural enough that those who have endured agony at the hands of wicked men should long with passion for that deliverance which demonstrates that faith was not in vain. What the soul covets is the opportunity to exclaim with the like-minded and the similarly beleaguered the words which close the prayer. It is God's sudden and undeniable intervention, His swift, not tardy defence of the righteousness and justice inseparable from His Person, which the weary heart covets, and who can deny the inevitability and reality of such desire even in a context of Christian prayer? Perhaps the Christian suppliant should not too strongly entertain such sentiments. He must in all such matters remember that his Lord prayed for those who drove the nails through His living flesh. At the same time He uttered no prayer for the mocking priests.

# 36

**Read Psalm 36; Proverbs 12**

## Occasion and author

The authorship is traditionally ascribed to David, and the sentiments and language support the claim. No particular occasion can be named.

## Commentary

**1–4** An ancient textual difficulty turns upon the alternatives 'his heart' and 'my heart' (1). From the Septuagint to the RSV the former has been chosen for its easier sense. Sin is personified. It indwells the ungodly as the Spirit of God inhabits those committed to Him. We have already seen that the heart is the Hebrew figure for the core of the personality. That which finds harbourage there permeates the whole being and captures the whole life. The wicked, having chosen his guest, becomes increasingly subject to the dominance of the 'thing' he entertains. It is of deep importance what we allow into the intimacy of mind and heart. 'Deep in his heart, sin whispers to the wicked man who cherishes no fear of God' (NEB). 'Sin lurks deep in the hearts of the wicked, forever urging them on to evil deeds' (1, LB). In all sin is deceit and the penalty which lies on all deceit is that the deceiver becomes his own victim. He imagines that iniquity can be concealed and controlled, unaware that the evil in the heart will seep through the whole mass of his person, made obvious and loathsome in every act, look, gesture (2), until he becomes no more himself but the helpless victim of his tolerated guest (3), unable, so complete is his damnation, to think of good even in the challenging quietness of the night (4). The progress of the tragedy is observed from v. 2 to v. 4. He imagines impunity, ceases to do good, plots evil and accepts the final fate. 'So set is he on his wrong courses that he rejects nothing evil' (NEB). Such is the descent to hell.

**5–9** This passage is Hebrew religious poetry at its best. The riot of the imagery is mystically satisfying. The writer may have pictured Hermon and the white ranges of Lebanon which lie beyond, enclosing the Beqaa. The poet is reaching high and low to picture the mercy, the righteousness, the justice of God. Man seems small in the presence of the great peaks. Stand in the Bernese Oberland under the uplifted snowfields of the Wetterhorn, the Jungfrau and the Eiger, or in the great valley of the Tasman Glacier, in the land where these words are written, under the mighty mass of Mount Cook . . . and man seems tiny, dwarfed, overwhelmed. So, for one who grasps a little of God's greatness, the Alpine stature of divine holiness. All human endeavour, human worth, is as nothing beneath it. Indeed, the vision might have been too daunting, had not the Almighty God made Himself known in Christ. Perhaps that is why vs. 7–9 return to earth and in imagery less overwhelming show man a guest in a great house, accepted, comforted and entertained.

**10–12** Therefore the child of God's care may trust his Lord for safety even in a world where evil can take the form and shape of men and find tongue, hands and feet in those who lend themselves to such using. Doom awaits evil and those who choose evil choose evil's fate, for evil is helpless unless it find incarnation in a surrendered person.

**Read Psalm 37; 1 John 2.1–17**

**Occasion and author**

The principle has already been established that, without compelling reasons to the contrary, the traditional authorship is accepted. The argument that such psalms as this have within them an element of 'wisdom literature' has no weight whatever. At what point is the utterance of wisdom to be distinguished from the language of piety and of worship? By what subtle dissection can the speech of heart and mind be separated? The psalm is well known, the fruit of mature pondering on the ways of God, a timeless piece of writing worthy of committal to the memory. The psalm calls for absolute trust, and on the principle of Paul's word to Philippi (3.1) makes its point by varied repetition. And, as someone has remarked, is there a better aid to memory than 'the cadenced monotony of the same idea cast into song'?

**Commentary**

**1,2** The verb employed (as in vs. 7, 8 and Prov. 24.19) means literally 'do not burn yourself up'. Rotherham renders: 'Burn not with vexation because of evildoers.' It is difficult amid the godless throng, in a world where evil appears triumphant, confident, arrogant and immune, not to feel the heat of anger. Truth on the scaffold, wrong on the throne, and a silent heaven, seem so often the experience of impatient man. The 'doers of iniquity', as Malachi said (3.15), are not to be envied. It is the end, in all situations, which counts. Croesus told Cyrus, in the famous story in Herodotus (1.98,99) that no man should lightly be counted happy until his life was ended. The evil denizens of this world, as God views time, are like the grass in lands where summer is hot.

**3** Trust therefore in God. Believe that He can overrule circumstances, transform evil, govern the heart, direct the mind, order the life. Meanwhile, awaiting perhaps what seems the tardy movement of His hand, 'do good'. There is always some task near the hand, always something creative, beneficent, worthy with which to fill in the time. And that task, well done, may prove to be a contribution to the whole situation. To 'dwell in the land' has more than a geographical significance. It can mean, for those whose prayer tangles with this psalm, the blessedness of dwelling within the circle of God's will. Nor is being fed a matter of bread and meat and the body's material needs. The Lord Himself stressed this truth (Matt. 4.4). The mind and the heart require their sustenance; all are part of the satisfaction God provides.
**4** Hence the call to take pleasure in doing God's will. Service, as the quotation from Malachi showed, can be dour – the obedience of the Prodigal's elder brother – and such service carries no promise. What are the desires of the heart? Not the passing whim, the ephemeral ambition, the unwise wish prompted by passing folly or misguided emotion. We have seen that Hebrew uses 'the heart' for the core of the personality, the real self, the seat and habitation of our God. What, faced by Christ in visible presence, would we ask for? So much of that which we innocently and quite legitimately pray for would fall away. We should be reduced to reality. Surely the heart's desire, when all else is done, is for God's blessed will in our lives. Let us continue by all means to petition as a child petitions a father, but let us expect the inevitable granting only of our true desires – His peace, His purpose, His strength.
**5,6** This involves the committal of the life. The word means utter trust, abandonment of the whole life in simple and unreserved faith to God Almighty. 'He will act', in such a case (as the RSV correctly translates). There is, however, virtue in the intruding pronoun of the old rendering (KJV) – 'and he will bring it to pass'. 'It' can, for all its monosyllabic brevity, represent that which matters most in any life. Let us, then, paraphrase the promise to this point: 'Trust God to take over your career, home, work, all the circumstances, aims and ambitions of life, and He will so mould events that your deepest and purest desires shall find unmeasured fulfilment and life will be filled with utter satisfaction. Furthermore (6), your life will be visibly a testimony to His grace, clear in its integrity as objects seen at midday.' Observe that the Hebrew for 'commit' is 'roll'. In Gen. 29.2 and 8, for example, it is used for rolling a stone cover on to a well. One can roll what one cannot lift, so the figure in the expression is an apt one.
**7,8** The verses are not repetitive. They stress the same truth, but approach from varied angles, and each shows a new facet. 'Be still' or 'be silent' is the precept of Isa. 26.3, and sums up much of what has already been said. The faithful must, in patience, stop fretting at the spectacle of apparently prosperous wickedness. The plans and plottings of evil, efficient, smoothly executed, seem to cry for action and no action seems to come, much less prevail, from man or God. This verse bids man to trust, to wait, to refrain from action. Observe, however, that this implies no withdrawal, no abandonment of battle. The sword does not sleep in the hands of the man who seeks to build a new Jerusalem. The psalmist has the heart's peace in view. He offers remedy against the frustration, the self-consuming anger, the dire

temptation to doubt of the man who finds the arrogant and victorious evil about him maddening.

**9–11** The mills of God are grinding and grinding exceeding small. To live long enough is to find illustration enough of the truth of the psalmist's confident prediction. Evil has never yet won the earth. If any ultimately win acceptance it is the gentle, the humble. The Lord graced this portion of the psalm by weaving it into the Beatitudes. Meekness is patience, forbearance, self-control. It is based on love, abstains from resentment and revenge. It is not weakness. The powerful and fiery Moses is described as 'a meek man'. He who is meek sides with Christ who shall one day reign. He enlists for the future. He will survive when violence has destroyed itself.

**12,13** True, the active malice of the wicked is a fact of life, but so is God, and, lifted from Psa. 2, comes the awesome figure of the laughter of God. It is strong Hebrew imagery and as a literary device who can deny the power of the juxtaposition of the gnashing teeth and hate-distorted face of man and the unimaginable sound of heaven's laughter?

**14,15** Toynbee has a long section in his famous *Study of History* called 'The Suicidalness of Militarism'. From his monumental knowledge of recorded civilizations, the great historian concludes that v. 15 can be illustrated from all the human story. Those that take the sword perish by the sword. Sometimes it requires a wider view of events than any one hour, or even any one observer's lifetime, provides, to demonstrate this fact, but fact it is.

**16–22** The language becomes that of 'wisdom literature' but, as any reader of the psalm who is not obsessed by categories can observe, the verses integrate with what has already been said. There is a natural progression of thought. The words are simple, the sentiments familiar, but the form of expression is designed to capture, contain and communicate important truth, and does so with vigour.

**23–34** The picture of the evil man is followed by the picture of the good linked to the opening movement of the psalm by the exhortation of v. 34. The whole of this portion of the psalm is the comparison, common enough in the Psalter and in Proverbs, of the good man and the bad. In a society salutarily preoccupied with ethics and behaviour it is common to find such definition clear and sharp. In societies in which values and standards crumble, and we know such societies too well for comfort, such distinctions blur and 'permissiveness' smudges the clear outline of the good and the bad.

**35,36** Touches of biography lighten the exposition. The 'green bay tree' (KJV) has won a place in the languages of men, and must not be lost to literature. Like many another mistranslation it has come to life. Translated literally, the phrase means a tree growing vigorously in its native soil.

The New English Bible translates: 'As a spreading tree in its native soil.' 'Like a cedar of Lebanon,' say both the RSV and the Jerusalem Bible (Moffatt is almost identical), and that is how the Jews of Alexandria put it, they who put the Old Testament into Greek so that the world could read it, in the third century before Christ.

The Lebanon cedar, growing on its native range behind the Phoenician coast, could be a 'green tree in its native soil'. So could a kauri in a New Zealand forest or a redwood in California. Or, if you will, a bay tree of Palestine. It is, after all, a native of Palestine, so can 'grow green in its native soil'. It likes the margins of brooks and streams and can reach a height of 60 feet, handsome in appearance among the stunted and weather-beaten trees which form, and formed in ancient times, too common a feature of land which was an early victim of the human vice of deforestation. It was this air of evergreen luxuriance which could make the *laurus nobilis*, the bay, a good candidate for the place in the English Bible which it has won.

Its qualities of proud luxuriance and its fate are shared by the Lebanon cedars, and, to the shame of both lands' pioneers, by the kauri and the redwood. The evergreens of this world seem to defy the storm and hide their inner decay, until the sudden day reveals it.

That, after all, is the theme of the psalm. Anyone who has seen the strutting tyrants of this century high on the stage before a shuddering world, knows that the psalmist's observation is true.

**37–40** The psalm has reached its climax, but, perhaps with the artistic desire of rounding off the alphabet (the psalm is acrostic, each pair of verses beginning with a letter of the Hebrew alphabet) the psalmist continues picking from the body of the psalm truths to be stressed again and emphasized.

## Conclusion

There is little general comment remaining. The psalmist has drawn his own conclusions. The man who trusts God is secure. He lives in another dimension where the eternal, the omniscient, the altogether good overflow the patterns of time. 'The world and all its passionate desires,' wrote John, 'will one day disappear. But the man who is following God's will is part of the permanent and cannot die' (1 John 2.17; J. B. Phillips).

# Read Psalm 38

## Occasion and author

The title 'for the memorial offering' (RSV) should read rather 'to bring to remembrance' (cf. Num. 5.15), and the psalm, as this ascription suggests, is an appeal to God to remember, and therefore to act. It is the third of the psalms listed as 'penitential' (6, 32, 51, 102, 130, 143 are the others) and must mark some occasion of almost unbearable physical and mental agony. Sickness of body accompanies sickness of soul and it is impossible to locate in David's recorded story any set of circumstances which could have evoked so passionate a cry for relief.

**Commentary**

**1–8** The psalm falls into three portions and each one opens with an appeal for aid. The language could hardly be more vivid, and the wild words of Job are the only parallel. There is no doubt at all that suffering has followed sin (3) and folly (5). It often does (John 5.14) but it is not for the onlooker to make the diagnosis (John 9.3). It was David's saving quality that he could face, confess and repudiate his sin. He feels like a thrashed and broken offender (1), a writhing victim of an archer's volley, struck down by a powerful hand (2), burdened (4), bereaved (6), fevered (7), exhausted (7) and in pain intolerable (8). It would be difficult to make the language of misery and suffering stronger.

**9–14** As though in a sudden outburst of faith the sufferer clings to the thought that God at least knows the bitter, weary way he treads, and that the sound of his sighing reaches His ears, but the besieging pain and all that it involves rush in again to sweep away all peace. There were those who saw his awful visitation of agony as divine judgement, and superstitiously withdrew. Job's friends, for all the inadequacy of their comfort, at least sat with him. Now, relatives included, they retreated from a spectacle so frightening. His enemies, sharpest blow of all, took a malicious delight in the situation and even thought to promote his trouble. The words almost echo Isa. 53 and Psa. 22. Conscious of his guilt (3–5), desperately reaching out in faith (9, 15), the sufferer tries to close his ears to the babble of malice, and guard his tongue. The Lord kept silence (Isa. 53.7), and it is sometimes the path of humility and dignity to treat uttered evil with the closed lips of steadfast rebuke.

**15–22** David, as his record shows, had learned to wait. Perhaps it was v. 15 which prompted the rabbinical editor to place this psalm of rejection and of pain in this position in the book. But, well though the difficult lesson had been learned, gusts of doubt and temptation still tried resolution. His foot has slipped. He is truly exposed to his enemies, but he trusts that his divine helper will regard his penitence and shield him (16). The thought prompts a new cry of pain and contrition (17,18) and a touch of fear (19). He wants, whatever the past, only good. Derek Kidner aptly quotes on this verse John 15.18,19. If a man, beset by sin, even obviously marred by sin, sets out to resist sin, it is not only his failures which stir the derision of the world. His very choice of good, his declared resistance to evil, inconsistently rouses the wrath and hatred of the weak, the wicked and the base. The fight, at times, seems lonely. Hence the closing words (21, 22).

**Conclusion**

This is a psalm for the darkest days. Paul tells the Ephesians so to wear and so to use the panoply of God that 'even when you have fought to a standstill you may still stand your ground'. Such a stand calls for all a man has of faith, courage and endurance, and life sometimes demands them all. The pain, the fear, the doubt which haunt the background are best faced, put into words, and exposed to God alone.

# 39

**Read Psalm 39; Job 7**

## Occasion and author

The psalm is clearly a companion piece born of the same mood and suffering as its predecessor. There are some of those verbal echoes which sometimes seem to prompt the placing of a psalm (e.g. 38.15, 39,7; 38.13, 39.9; 38.11, 39.10). Perhaps the same problem, the same stress of mind which drew from the sufferer the agony of the preceding psalm, has quietened a little, but not passed from memory or consciousness. The pain is remembered with a small measure of tranquillity.

## Commentary

**1** The sufferer has taken care not to complain before the hostile world. He has remembered that 'the Canaanite and the Perizzite dwell in the land' (Gen. 13.7) and that a watching world judges a man's God by his behaviour under stress.

**2** On the other hand, the sufferer recognizes that the suppression involved has harmed him. an acute psychological diagnosis.

**3** The pressure grew until he found the relief of prayer. When he spoke it was to God. Possibly the preceding psalm (38) was the flood of speech, confession and contrition which at this point was released, and the rest of the psalm, a more reflective prayer on the meaning and the brevity of life, was not the utterance described in the last words of this verse. This is a mere suggestion, but if the two psalms are linked it could make biographical sense.

**4–6** A quiet reflective prayer follows. Whatever drew forth the preceding psalm led the sufferer to face the brevity and frailty of life. It has been the theme of man's most wistful longings. 'Creatures of a day,' wrote Pindar of Thebes five centuries before Christ, 'what are we? The dream of a shadow, such is man.' And Euripides of Athens, half a century later in a haunting chorus:

*If any far-off state there be*
*Dearer to life than mortality,*
*The hand of death hath hold thereof,*
*And mists are under and mists above.*
*The other life is a fountain sealed,*
*The depths below us are unrevealed,*
*And we float on legends for ever.*

Without 'some sure word of God', as Socrates said fifty years later still, what is there for man to say?

Hence the imagery of transience which haunts the writers of the Bible. 'For they shall soon be cut down like the grass and wither as the green herb . . . In the morning they are like grass which grows up. In the morning it flourishes and springs up; in the evening it is mown down and withers . . . My heart is smitten like grass and withers . . . As for man his days are as grass . . . for the wind passes over it and it is gone.' So the psalmist (Pss. 37.2; 90.5,6; 102.4,11; 103.15). The chance tuft of green which sprang with the early rains on the tiled rooftop, and perished with even greater promptitude when the sun baked the shallow pocket of mould, provides a refinement of the image. 'Let them be like the grass on the housetops, which withers before it grows up,' runs Psa. 129.6.

Isaiah follows (40.6–8), catching up the psalmist's imagery and adding the characteristic touches of his rich poetry:

*All flesh is grass,*
*and all its beauty is like the flower of the field.*
*The grass withers, the flower fades,*
*when the breath of the Lord blows upon it;*
*surely the people is grass.*
*The grass withers, the flower fades . . .*

It runs like a ballad refrain and caught the imagination of man. Seven centuries after Isaiah, James paraphrased it: '. . . like the flower of the grass he will pass away. For the sun rises with its scorching heat and withers the grass . . .' (1.10,11).

The Old Testament, as more than one context in the psalms suggests, had a clearer notion of immortality than some are ready to grant, but it was the resurrection of Christ which gave final form and shape to the hope of another life. Hence the pathos of this prayer.

**7–11** And hence the need for vindication here, now, for deliverance visible and sure from the power of sin and the 'scorn of the fool' (8), from obvious punishment patiently endured (9,10).

**12,13** The sadness of the ending is poignant. Whatever hope David may at times have entertained about another life (for example 23.6) it has faded here. There is little to distinguish his sad words from those of the little poem written a millennium later by the cultured emperor Hadrian who built the great wall across Britain. Here are the lines as Geoffrey Household translates them:

*Odd little comrade, comfortable guest,*
*Capricious elfin puff of air,*
*You're off? But where? And when you've left my breast,*
*Tense little traveller, pale and bare,*
*Will you find anything to laugh at there?*

'Little to distinguish', should we say? Only this – the psalmist, in a sort of blind hope, like Job, clings to God, and prays for all that he can understand,

God's intervention at least in the context which he knows, this life, this world with all its pain, its contradictions, its seeming desolation. One step away was the projection of the thought of God's justice into the claim of immortality. As Tennyson put it again and again, this life cannot be all:

*Thou wilt not leave us in the dust:*
*Thou madest man, he knows not why,*
*He thinks he was not made to die;*
*And thou hast made him: thou art just.*

*Truth for truth and good for good!*
*The Good, the True, the Pure, the Just –*
*Take the charm 'For ever' from them,*
*And they crumble into dust.*

*Not only cunning casts in clay:*
*Let Science prove we are, and then*
*What matters Science unto men,*
*At least to me? I would not stay.*

**Conclusion**

The New Testament provides it. 'If then the proclamation is that Christ has risen from the dead, how do some of you say that there is no resurrection from the dead? If there is no resurrection from the dead, neither is Christ risen. If Christ be not risen, our gospel is without content, and your faith as empty. And we are proved false witnesses of God, because our testimony was that He did raise up Christ, and, if indeed the dead are not raised up, He did not raise Christ. For if the dead are not raised, I repeat, neither is Christ risen. And if Christ be not risen, your faith is useless, you are still in your sins. Those too who "fell asleep in Christ" are dead and gone. If only in this life we have hope in Christ we are of all men most to be pitied' (1 Cor. 15. 12–19).

But let us admire the valour of the sad sufferer of the psalm whose faith in God's goodness stood with no clear grasp of such a hope.

## Read Psalm 40; Jeremiah 38.6–13

### Occasion and author

There is again no compelling reason to reject the traditional authorship. Indeed the five psalms which close the first book of the Psalter form a sequence. The theme of waiting for God's certain intervention and vindication is set forth in Psa. 37. The next psalm speaks of an agonizing experience which put such principles to the test. The remaining three psalms of the group show a gradual emergence from the time and experience of testing, and the return, with faith tried and hardened in affliction's fire, to the truths enunciated in the first of the series. These five psalms form a book of prayer for any Christian passing through some dark night of the soul's experience.

### Commentary

**1** A Hebrew infinitive construction, designed for emphasis, is used here. It might roughly be rendered 'waiting I waited'. The NEB with the repeated verb perhaps renders it best: 'I waited, waited for the Lord.' Hebrew is not rich in adverbs and adjectives, and it is sometimes effective in translation to try a more literal rendering than to supply a word like 'patiently'. The NEB continues: 'He bent down to me', which avoids the suggestion of a detached awareness of the suppliant's presence implied by the KJV, and RSV renderings. Moffatt's: 'He turned and listened to my cry' is not so good.

**2** The metaphor is best understood in the light of Jeremiah's experience. That of Joseph was similar. The bottle-shaped cisterns cut into the rock were not uncommon in the land. Fractured by earth movements or emptied by drought, they provided rough places of confinement or torture. The split cistern provided Jeremiah with a figure for apostasy (2.13) and the picture was no doubt stamped upon his mind by the awful experience he endured. The well would be deep in mud and slime and the victim would slip and struggle, unable to stand, until exhaustion or suffocation ended his misery. From such a pit of filth and peril, like Jeremiah, the psalmist saw himself rescued by a saviour's intervention. At last firm rock was beneath his feet and a path surveyed before him. God, the psalmist found, does more than rescue, He rehabilitates, makes secure, provides a way to tread.

**3** A man cannot flounder in the mud, and be silent on the rock. Saved, the redeemed man finds a new song (Rev. 7.9–12). The 'new song' is perhaps the poem which runs from v. 4 to v. 11. On the other hand every human being is unique. No fingerprint, or recorded voice pattern is identical with any other. The very physical formula, the molecular structure of each man and woman is unique. So, too, is the history of each person's spiritual experience and relationship with God. It follows that all men, if they will but sing it, have each a new song, each a peculiar task, each a function in life which no one else can fulfil.

**4–6** The new song of the psalmist begins here and links forthwith trust in God and separation from evil men (2 Cor. 6.14–17; Rom. 12.2). Indeed one might suppose that Paul had this passage in mind when he wrote to the Roman Church. 'Please (his opening verb means "please" in modern Greek), please, brothers, bearing in mind the mercies (5) of God, offer yourselves a living sacrifice (6), holy, the sacrifice God desires, the only service you can really give. Stop trying to make yourselves like the society you live in (4) . . .' What is said of sacrifice has many echoes in the Old Testament, and David, no doubt, had in mind the rebuke to Saul (1 Sam. 15.22), and Isaiah possibly had this passage in mind (1.11).

**7,8** Hebrews 10.5–10 interprets this whole passage messianically but this majestic role accorded it does not exclude its original and personal meaning. David comes, in view of God's multiplied mercies (5), to offer himself 'a living sacrifice' (Rom. 12.1). The dedication is to God and to his appointed task and the two can never be separated. The 'book' could be the roll of the coronation decree, if such there was, or the book of the Law which the king of Israel was bound to observe (cf. 2 Kings 22.13). In the New Testament interpretation the word assumes a grander meaning (Luke 24.27; John 5.46).

**9–11** The new song ends with a quiet ending after the fashion of Greek lyrics. The psalmist presents his poem, an offering of praise. Verse 11 is a statement of fact (NEB), not a plea for help (RSV).

**12–17** And then, as though he pictures himself in the sanctuary, the choir now silent and the multitude departing, the psalmist imagines a pause. He stands alone near the place of song. His heart has risen at his own words thus rendered. In the emptying courtyard he turns to private prayer, for the last tremors of his suffering, the pain that has taught lessons so deep, are still felt in recent memory. The roofs of the city are below. The people throng the streets, each an island of his own joys and sorrows, love and hate, each one known to God alone. How safe was the future, how loyal, after all, the many who made up the city throng? He had known, in the sudden revelation brought in the day of his pain and sickness, that many lay in wait, with small affection for their king. Their king? How poor and needy (17) after all was he, a fragile thing of flesh, his frailty demonstrated in his sickness and distress. Let God, his only hope, preserve.

### Conclusion

The last verses are repeated with minor changes in Psa. 70, but the oldest literary and textual evidence shows no conflation here. If the dramatic interpretation suggested here be accepted, the psalm as a united whole makes sense, indeed striking sense.

**Read Psalm 41**

**Occasion and author**

The psalm is by the same hand as those which precede it. The phrase 'poor and needy' is picked up from the closing verse of the preceding psalm and evokes a personal memory. It is woven biographically into a conclusion to the whole book. The writer's mind goes back to the days of his dire illness and there is a touch of drama in the presentation which should hold the reader's imagination alert.

**Commentary**

**1–5** God alone was 'this poor man's' only worthy sick visitor. See the marginal translation of the last phrase of v. 3 (RSV); 'Thou changest all his bed'. The Jerusalem Bible, rendering the word 'all', translated it 'most carefully you make his bed when he is sick'.

**6–12** If a guess be hazarded concerning the occasion, it could be that this is one of the psalms of the Absalom rebellion. Perhaps serious illness and visible loss of physical capacity gave the rebel prince food for his propaganda and opportunity to plot. David had too easily become an eastern king, remote from his people and lonely in his power and his pain. He had not realized the alienation of his court until the occasion of his sickness made him suddenly aware of hypocrisy, ill-concealed dislike, and malicious impatience with his presence in the place of rule.

**13** The benediction to Book One, or doxology, perhaps written by the editor of the psalms. If so, it shows in the warmth of his piety how much the book has moved him. It is a book full of pain, as it is full of faith and confidence in God's love. It is a rounded collection largely from the pen of David. Perhaps intentionally, it began and ended with a cluster of psalms written in the days of David's suffering over Absalom, his rejection and his restoration.

# 42,43

**Read Psalms 42,43;**
**Jeremiah 14.1–6**

## Occasion and author

There is a good reason to take these two psalms as one. The repetition of the refrain of the former at the close of the latter poem, and the coincidences of thought and language, are striking. This alone might not be good cause for conflating the two pieces were the internal evidence not supported by the external evidence. Many manuscripts run the two psalms together and one ancient authority speaks of 147 psalms in the Psalter. This implies a division of three psalms into two, perhaps with the idea of a tidy 150 in all. On the other hand, the Septuagint sets the psalms down separately. The author is unknown but he appears to have in mind the northern parts of Transjordan, the Golan Heights, running up into the foothills of Hermon and the associated Anti-Lebanon range. Guesses at identity have varied. The road to Damascus, and round the curve of the Fertile Crescent, lies that way. Was the lamentation that of Jehoiakim on his way to Babylonian exile, the cry of a priest banished by Athaliah, or the poem of a Levite looking back at the last landscape of his native land? The clue takes us no further.

## Commentary

**1** Whoever the writer was, he was a sensitive man attuned to the suffering of the animal creation. There is no chase involved in spite of the three-century-old version of the psalm by Nahum Tate and Nicholas Brady . . .

*As pants the hart for cooling streams*
*When heated in the chase.*

The scene is one of drought with the sun a burden on a hot, arid land, the very landscape which lies north-east of the Golan on a blazing summer day. With similar sensitivity and compassion for suffering creatures of the wilderness, Jeremiah, another exile, drew his vivid picture of drought . . .

*The hind on the moor calves and abandons*
*For the grass has not come.*
*On the bare heights stand the wild asses,*
*Gasping for air*
*With glazen eyes –*
*Herb there is none.*

Perhaps Cowper knew this verse, when he saw himself 'a stricken deer'.

**2** Fierce thirst, and the benediction of the water which quenches it, are intensely real in the Bible. In Genesis the herdsmen of the patriarchs strive with the alien for the wells laboriously cut in the hot rock. In Exodus the panic of thirst shakes and threatens Moses' leadership. Psalmists and prophets liken joy, happiness, life itself, God's grace, to the blessed stream and the fountain filled. At Sychar, and in the Temple court, the Lord likens water to eternal life; on the Mount He promises fulfilment only to those who thirst for righteousness, and the words are caught up by the closing pages of the Bible.

It requires an effort of the imagination, indeed it requires some sharing of experience, for dwellers in other lands to apprehend the strength and vividness of the image. Goran Schildt writes vividly of the mill-pond below Delphi where he bathed on a burning day: 'Cool, fresh, crystal-clear water,' he says, 'only those who have known drought and heat in a land where the sunshine feels like a physical weight, a rain of molten gold in which you walk hunched up, more eagerly on the look-out for shelter than in the heaviest downpour, only those who have known the southern summer can understand what water is.'

The verse vibrates with man's instinctive longing for infinitude, surely a mark of the stamp of God's image upon him. Plato, that greatest mind among the Greeks, ever reaching out for perfection, that 'pattern stored in the heavens' of which all that is good on earth could only be pale reflection; Job, in his darkness, crying out for God . . . the quest haunts all history. Nothing which has limits satisfies. Perfect justice, perfect beauty, righteousness unsoiled, man ever reaches for them. And the writer of the psalm, stumbling through the heat, longs for God, sobbing out his frustration as the cruel captors sneer at his indomitable faith.

**3** For sneer they do. They did at Calvary: 'Eloi, Eloi, lama sabachthani' – 'Stop, let's see whether Elijah will come to save Him.' It is a hard world. It censures grief as lack of faith, it theorizes over agony like Job's friends, it taunts misfortune as proof of atheism. 'Continually' they scoffed, for evil is persistent. The sufferer is vulnerable because he has openly confessed his faith.

**4** And that is why he fixes his memory on the past. He remembers in the darkness what God taught him in the light. The image in the mind had its pain. He had moved with the marching crowd on such occasions as those which brought the worshippers to the Temple mount, such as those for whose singing Pss. 120–134 were written. What a mockery of such a caravan was that which stumbled on in the burning sun with Hermon blue and hard against the sky.

**5–7** There is strength in the thought, and in a dialogue with himself the psalmist challenges his despair. 'Disquieted' is a strong word. It is used in 46.3, of the tossing and raging of the sea, and somewhere in the landscape of the psalm the image may be real, for the poet may be remembering a storm-tossed Galilee. He could have looked down on the great oval of water from the Golan Heights if he passed up to the plateau from the Yarmuk, or if he went up the western shore, the waters could have been in wide view from hill and lakeshore before the road swung across the upper Jordan and up the hills above the sources of the Jordan. A gale, roaring south down the Rift

Valley, can turn the waters, as the Gospels record, into boiling turmoil. Such was the tumult of his soul. Verse 7 picks up the image and varies it, as though the waves in wild emulation responded each to each with hiss, and crash, and roaring.

**8** 'Commands' is a curious word, as though God ordered His love to come like the Comforter and touch the fevered mind with calm, a harmony invading the heart and eliciting a confident prayer. God, says Job (35.10), 'gives songs in the night'. It calls for faith to hear such music but they are blessed whose ear is so attuned.

**9–43.5** The psalm has said what it has to say. The full explanation still eludes the mind, but the heart is at rest. Why the agony has been permitted is still a question which calls for an answer, and man, caught and buffeted by life, has the right to seek such elucidation. And this the more so when vindication before a sneering, hostile world is the goal. The longing for light and truth (3) is a fundamental outreaching of the soul. Both lead to the habitation of the Lord.

**Conclusion**

Perhaps the brave writer's personal battle with despair is the lesson, the daunting lesson, in this passionate prayer. He has found his way home. Antoinette Goetschius, the American poet, writes:

*When I am sore beset I seek some quiet place,*
*Some lonely room or barren windswept hill,*
*And there in silence wait until*
*I see again the smile upon God's face.*

*I feel again his presence fill me like the dawn*
*And hear once more his whispered 'Peace, be still',*
*And know again the strength to do his will,*
*I turn to take my load and find it gone . . .*

And on hope, J. J. S. Perowne quotes: 'There are hours when physical suffering darkens the windows of the soul; days in which shattered nerves make life simply endurance; months and years in which intellectual difficulties, pressing for solution, shut out God. Then faith must be replaced by hope. "What I do you know not now, but you shall know hereafter" . . .' It is useless looking elsewhere than Godwards. All else, at such times, is bent, distorted.

**Read Psalm 44; Romans 8.18–39**

**Occasion and author**

This is named as a song of the sons of Korah written by a poet among these Temple custodians of hymn and music, or set in order by them. When it was written is another matter. Some have ascribed it to times of trouble in the days of the early kingdom, when David was beset along all his eastern frontiers by the Syrians, Edomites and Ammonites, with a restless Philistia in his rear. The psalm, however, to a sensitive ear, does not sound Davidic. At the other extreme, led by the claim in the psalm to national faithfulness, Calvin, and many who have followed him, set the psalm in the days of the Maccabees. There are two objections to this late dating. In the first chapter of the stirring books of the Maccabees, widespread apostasy among Hellenized Jews is alleged. True, it was part of the ruthless purging of the national leaders that such deviation was suppressed. There is, however, the weightier objection that so late a composition might not have found its way into the canon of Scripture.

**Commentary**

**1–8** The situation is obviously disastrous. Indeed, at risk of fruitlessly adding to the suggested dates, one might refer to Habakkuk's passionate first chapter and ask whether Nebuchadnezzar's trampling of the nation might not have prompted this psalm. The theme confronts a major problem. Why do the good suffer? Is all distress punishment for sin? . . . In times past, as history witnessed, the nation had received its just reward. They gave God their trust. God moved before His people. He is still their God. Then let Him do as the old sagas claimed He once had done – arise and scatter the victorious foe, be it Antiochus Epiphanes or any other intruder who sought to attack God in attacking God's people. Such had been the content and the proclamation (8) of old faith. Could God be other than He had been?

**9–16** Had God changed? Instead of victory there was defeat, and more than defeat, spoliation, massacre, deportation, slavery, the contempt of the heathen, laughing, and shame. Jews all through history have known the reality of this cry of bewilderment and pain. Jews died building the Colosseum, slaves from the Great Rebellion. Some Jew of the same captive multitude scrawled SODOMA GOMORRA on the wall in Pompeii, when the town died under the hot ash of Vesuvius on the afternoon of August 24, A.D. 79.

**17–22** Worse. Calamity seemed to contradict the Covenant (e.g. Lev. 26 and Deut. 28). They bowed under the chastisement of God when they recognized its retribution, when the blows fell in accordance with the sanctions contained in the Mosaic Law. Now it was different. This catastrophe had come at a time of faithfulness, when no idolatry was defiling the land, when devotion was sincere, unspoiled by secret rebellion which could not escape the penetrating eye of God (21). The writer speaks within the context of the Law's formal righteousness, but of his conviction there can be no doubt. The nation, for whom he writes this national prayer, has done its part. Why has not God done His? Then in the last verse a glimpse of a deeper truth appears. All suffering is not chastisement. God does not always 'send' trial and pain upon His people as crude and unfeeling theologies are accustomed to maintain. God allows, God in His wisdom permits, the native and endemic evil of the world to sweep around the Christian. It engulfed Christ. It nailed Him to the cross. It is because the loyal follower of God is committed to his stance, that his troubles often come. Paul caught up this verse and gave it precisely that interpretation in Rom. 8.36. The verse approaches the Christian realization. To accept Christ is to take up the cross. To take sides in the vast struggle of good against evil is to meet the battle wounds of a conflict in which God, if 'God was in Christ', is Himself involved. The pain demonstrates, not the choice or tolerance of evil, but the acceptance and promotion of the good.

**23–26** Bold he approaches the eternal throne. No one who has known the dark hours of the soul and the battle-strain of life will be shocked at the frankness and forthright language of this prayer. This is the boldness of faith, and when such thoughts invade the mind, it is better to have them out in words, to rid the soul of them, and leave God to extract the meaning His love can discern behind the clumsy speech of man. The psalm ends with reference to God's steadfast love. It is a pointer to Paul's comment in Rom. 8.37: 'In these things we are more than conquerers . . .'

**Conclusion**

Treat this poem gently. Sadness, despair, perplexity, equally with happiness and joy, can be offerings to God. No one, as God taught the 'comforters' of Job, has a right to probe and analyse the deep levels of another's grief, much less to comment unsympathetically on the manner in which the sufferer pours it into words. Johnson was right when he said:

*Of all the griefs that harass the distressed*
*Sure the most bitter is the scornful jest.*

But equal, surely, is the one who, without having passed through waters and cataracts as deep, makes another's pain a theme of exhortation. Ezekiel, hot against the shattered exiles, found a dumbness fall on him. 'I sat where they sat,' he says, and there is often nothing else for the loving friend to do. It is the worst of crudity to 'patch grief with proverbs', as Shakespeare put it. And it was the same poet who made Juliet cry:

*Is there no pity sitting in the clouds*
*That sees into the bosom of my grief?*

He who knows Christ knows the answer to that question.

**Read Psalm 45; John 2**

### Occasion and author

This is an epithalamium or marriage hymn of which examples exist in Greek and Latin literature. Catullus, 'tenderest of Roman poets,' as Tennyson called him, has left us a beautiful example of such writing. It is therefore a piece written to order, a laureate ode, but one which, as the opening verse shows, enlisted the full co-operation of the writer.

C. S. Lewis remarks: 'We are nowadays surprised to find that such an official piece of work, made to order by a court poet for a special occasion, should be good poetry. But in ages when the arts had their full health, no one would have understood our surprise. All the great poets, painters and musicians of old could produce great work "to order". One who could not would have seemed as great a humbug as a captain who could not navigate, or a farmer who could only farm when the fit took him.'

Conjecture can roam widely concerning the prince and princess involved. There are limitations. The Davidic court must surely be the royal context of the poem, and this rules out the suggestion of Ahab's and Jezebel's marriage. Jezebel's daughter, Athaliah, who married Jehoram, son of Jehoshaphat, could, however, be a possibility. This could account for the reference to the gold trade with Ophir, an unsuccessful venture of Jehoshaphat's in his distant emulation of Solomon. And Ahab, father of Athaliah, had a palace lavishly panelled in ivory. The objection that Jehoram, not to mention Athaliah, provided in later years some grim pages of history, has little weight. Too many mornings of sunshine in marriage and in royal reigns have ended in darkness and gloom.

### Commentary

**1** 'My heart is stirred by a noble theme,' he cries (NEB). Poetry can begin nowhere else if it is to be more than tinkling cymbal and sounding brass. He is to write of the king and the king has his whole soul's admiration. The Hebrew lacks the article which translators insist on inserting. 'I write,' he says, 'for a king.' Could one have a theme more regal?

**2–5** Physical beauty is matched by grace of speech and both are signs of uncommon favour. The psalmist then calls for strength of arm to defend his people. 'Send her victorious, happy and glorious . . .' we sing without thought of sanguinary aggression. Judah lived, has always lived, behind frontiers of fear. There has never been a time when the little land had anything other than a ring of hostile borderlands and the sea behind. A leader who could provide his people with security was a necessity. Truth, meekness and righteousness (4), however, governed his prowess, and under such moral limitations war, for war's sake, self-exalting imperialism, can hardly find a place in ambition or in policy.

**6–7** Heb. 1.8,9 boldly refers these verses to Christ, and no adjusting of translation can make the author of the psalm say anything other than the writer of Hebrews, following the translators of the Septuagint, understood him to say. How, then, does this conform to the primary purpose of the psalm? Obviously the whole poem does not refer to Christ, and the sudden intrusion of one manifestly messianic verse appears to distort a sense which would otherwise have been smooth and uninterrupted. Does the writer, in an overflow of eloquence, address the royal bridegroom as God? This is not a context of king-worship, such as many a pagan nation of that place and time practised. One can follow Derek Kidner's remark and speak of the language 'bursting its banks' and demanding something more than its primary significance, that overflow of meaning caught and authorized by the writer of Hebrews. Or, perhaps, in a surge of exalted insight, the poet sees the king as a prefigurement of the Incarnation, a transient occupant of a throne which symbolized a mightier royalty, and the bearer of a weighty responsibility to be Another than himself and act as that Other would.

**8,9** The poetry is back to earth with a picture of the king in full regalia. He has been set forth as a man, a warrior and a ruler. Now it is the bridegroom on the wedding day. Cassia is perfume from the aromatic bark of a tree. Ezek. 27.19 speaks of it as a product of the Tyrian trade, one of the luxury goods from the Phoenicians, introduced into the land by Solomon, and after the division of the land imported by the Israelite kingdom and perhaps re-exported to Jerusalem. Or perhaps the resumption of overseas merchandising under Jehoshaphat, if such was the occasion, had brought back a touch of Phoenician luxury with the daughter of a Phoenician queen to the more austere Jerusalem court. Aloes is a similar botanical product of rarity and value, derived from the heartwood of an Eastern tree. It found its way west from India or beyond. The poet is gaining his coloured effect after Masefield's fashion in *Cargoes*, by piling words of emotive force and association. So too with ivory. Ahab's palace was panelled with flakes of ivory (1 Kings 22.39) and the practice was castigated by Amos as a sign of reprehensible luxury (3.15; 6.4). Megiddo and Samaria in particular have yielded a wealth of ivory objects.

**9** Gold of Ophir, Arabia Felix, land of gold and incense, adorned the queen, who, with the royal attendants, her ladies-in-waiting, made part of the picture.

**10** The camera turns, as it were, and focuses on the princess. Hers is a strong duty. She leaves one royal court for another and must make the firm choice, the choice of Rebecca in the beautifully told story of Gen. 24. She has donned another allegiance for there is a parting and a beginning in all marriage – a truth which still holds. Marriage lacks an ingredient if old ties are allowed damagingly to conflict with new. A couple edgy about the family they leave to begin a new one, has tolerated a source of friction which might so easily be blocked. To be together, a new unit, objectively to view the problems which unwise parents can sometimes occasion, is a strong force for trust and confidence in a newly established family.

**11–17** There is abundant reward in new royal standing and influence, the pomp of state, a nation's respect, the gladness of love, the joy of children and a name to be remembered – not unworthy ambitions, provided they are held with humility and meekness, the gifts of God, the source of benefaction, and the ingredients of a respect based on esteem and popularity founded on love.

### Conclusion

It is wrong to regard this psalm as a prefiguring of Christ, except for v. 6 where the language is inexplicable without a transcendent meaning – as wrong as it is to distort the Song of Songs into an allegory of Christ and the Church, an old interpretation which sensitive people find acutely repellent. Set this psalm with the Song, and with the wedding feast of Cana as God's benediction on human love and marriage, and even on those joyous expressions of such happiness in ceremony, in adornment and pomp.

**Read Psalm 46; Revelation 21.9–27**

### Occasion and author

No one can tell the historical circumstances which led to this song of Korah. Some mighty menace had evaporated. A peril on the embattled frontiers had passed away. It could have been when Sennacherib's tide of war rolled wondrously back. Isaiah, indeed, had compared the Assyrian invasion to a swollen river bursting all its banks. Isaiah, too, had compared the city of Jerusalem, an invested island in that sea of war, to a peaceful refuge with its own gently flowing Siloam stream (8.6). That small waterway was a stream which 'made glad the city of God'. To read Isa. 14.9–27; 33.21; 36 and 37, is almost to conclude that Isaiah wrote this psalm in 701 B.C. Conjecture, however, can go no further. Luther based his famous hymn 'A mighty Fortress is our God' on this psalm.

### Commentary

**1** All men need a refuge. A concordance will emphasize the frequency with which the word occurs. The need to escape, the desire to escape, is not to be dismissed under an emotive term – 'escapism'. It depends upon the peril to be avoided. It depends upon that to which escape is made. The coward runs away from that which he should in duty and uprightness face. The good man retreats from that which can mar and soil him. There are those who take craven refuge from life, its obligations and its demands, in drugs, drink and withdrawal. There are those who find their duty in the deepest involvement with life around them but who need, for their soul's health, to retreat to the 'higher Rock', to take refuge in God from perils worse than those which can come armed across any frontier. R. A. Torrey, most logical of this century's evangelists, had a famous sermon based on Isa. 28.15–17, in which he listed rebellious man's 'refuge of lies'. Finally, let us quote George Macdonald, C. S. Lewis' master: 'That man is perfect in faith who can come to God in the utter dearth of his feelings and desires, without a glow or an aspiration, with the weight of low thoughts, failures, neglects and wandering forgetfulness, and say to Him: "Thou art my refuge." '

**2,3** There are times in life when that which seemed most stable totters, and the changeful, the capricious, the tumultuous seem to engulf the truths, the standards, the institutions which seemed beyond all shaking. Such is the meaning of this vivid word-picture. Carmel and Hermon were monuments of stability in the land, but the whole coast had no peaceful haven. Man, from Ashkelon to Tyre, was ever at grips with the restless Mediterranean. Herod, by some of the mightiest maritime engineering that archaeology has brought to light, made a harbour for Rome at Caesarea, but the great sea-walls were always under attack. That is why the sea is almost always a metaphor of storm in the Bible. Even Galilee, which could lie calm and silver between its hills, could turn treacherously upon those who trusted it and become a cauldron of surf.

**4–7** The picture seems connected with Isaiah's reference to the Siloam stream, 'whose waters go softly' (8.6). It was a small, quiet rivulet, but Jerusalem's lifeline when the invasion beat on her walls. With infinite labour the menaced city had cut the famous Siloam tunnel to bring the life-giving flood inside the walls. God's help, the poet is saying, is like that, quiet, unobtrusive, sustaining. 'Like a river glorious is God's perfect peace . . .' Evil is noisy, tumultuous. God is silent. Jeremiah's raging cauldron in his opening vision, pictured the military menace from the north. The blossoming almond tree, God's answer, was set over against it. Verse 6, a complex of short, crashing clauses, the very picture of the world's upheaval, quietens into v. 7. The psalmist in his day had seen it. The strife-ridden world longs for some similar, wider, conclusive consummation. 'O that it were today', as the old hymn on the long-muted doctrine of the Second Coming prays.

**8–10** The words would assume ghastly significance if the occasion of the psalm was Sennacherib's disaster. The camp on which the bubonic plague seems to have fallen would have been a scene of awesome destruction when panic succeeding pandemic had done its grim work.

## Conclusion

Verse 11 is the conclusion. The psalm ends where it began – 'Rock of Ages cleft for me,' as a Christian might put it, 'let me hide myself in Thee'. A refuge must protect. Reality is the hail which sweeps away all 'refuges of lies'. A refuge must be near and God is 'very present'. As Moffatt puts it, 'we shall find him very near' when discouragement, trial and temptation flood upon us. 'Stop your striving,' R. K. Harrison translates v. 10, 'and recognize that I am God.' Moffatt, more boldly, says: 'Give in.'

**Read Psalm 47; 2 Samuel 6**

### Occasion and author

Speculation has been rife over this song of triumph. Was it an ode of jubilation over the fall of Sennacherib, over Jehoshaphat's defeat of the Eastern Gentile alliance (2 Chron. 20), a post-exilic hymn – or is it a companion piece to Psa. 24, a song of the sons of Korah to accompany the song of David? Who knows? If a choice must be made (and it is not necessary), the last suggestion is the most likely. It is good not to be dogmatic, however, where dogmatism is both unnecessary and even reprehensible. It is the triumph of Israel which makes the theme, and which constitutes the interest. The handful who remember Armistice Day (few can remember Mafeking), and the larger number who remember VE Day, and London's jubilation, may perhaps be the only ones alive who know what wild relief and uninhibited joy in victory can do to a population. This must be held in mind when the passionate sense of triumph which rings through this poem is assessed.

### Commentary

**1–9** There is small occasion to divide into verses and sections. It is the total impact of the psalm which is significant. Observe the phrase in the fifth verse: 'God has gone up with a shout.' It is the phrase of 2 Sam. 6.15, and is a point for the timing of the hymn. Verse 7 stands out. It is the vision of Abraham breaking through – One God and God of All. The vision overflows into the next two verses, the ideal which haunted Isaiah (14.1; 66.18). It is in this sense that the psalm is messianic, Pauline and universal. There is, in fact, in v. 9, a hint of Gentile proselytes. It is variously translated, but R. K. Harrison puts it: 'The nobles from pagan peoples assemble to be one with the people of the God of Abraham.' Was this a reference to such converts as Uriah the Hittite, and the man of Cush of 2 Sam. 18.21? We have no information from the period (whatever the period was) to determine the strength of this Gentile element in the population, but they were the forerunners of a host. The literal translation is 'the willing ones' and can be rendered 'nobles' or 'princes' as most versions do. But is the literal translation too readily overlooked – the volunteers, those who of their free will identify themselves with God's people? It is an intriguing thought, and touches the global vision of the psalm.

**Read Psalm 48; Isaiah 36, 37**

**Occasion and author**

Another hymn of the Korah hymnologists, and placed here because of the association of its theme with the preceding psalm. It is possible to hazard a guess that the piece was associated with the strange experience of Sennacherib's invasion, the horror and catastrophic passing of which colour so much of the early part of Isaiah and culminate in the vivid historical chapters in that prophecy. The poetry seems to envisage an army confronting and bypassing Jerusalem to find sudden panic and destruction. This is exactly what happened. The inroad of the Assyrians was a theme in their own inscriptions as it was in the records of the Old Testament. Siege, devastation and destruction flowed over Palestine. The horror of the invasion lives in Isa. 10 where the very route, marked by blazing and evacuated towns is described. But when the invader, who seems to have survived the disaster which fell on his army, spoke of Jerusalem his remarks (they are found on the Taylor Prism) become muted: 'Himself (Hezekiah) I shut up in his royal city, Jerusalem, like a bird in a cage. Earthworks I threw against him. Anyone coming out of the gate I turned back to his misery.' This looks very like an unsuccessful siege. The psalm fits such a deliverance and is usefully read in such a context.

**Commentary**

**1–3** Jerusalem is, in fact, imposingly placed. It stands high on its rocky ridge, a fine sight from the adjacent eminence of the Mount of Olives, majestically above for anyone toiling up the ascending roads from the Great Rift Valley. From any angle, it is, as Sennacherib himself described it, a royal city. It 'rises aloft in beauty' as the second verse says. Taylor's free version may catch the cryptic poetry of the words: 'What a glorious sight! See Mount Zion rising north of the city high above the plains for all to see – Mount Zion, joy of all the earth, the residence of the great King.' And then the NEB on v. 3: 'In her palaces God is known for a tower of strength.' The city, to the eyes of the delivered, seemed clad in new beauty. The acropolis of Zion, the royal residence, appeared a very throne of God, especially in view of Hezekiah's triumphant faith – the supreme gift of the valiant Isaiah to his king.

**4–8** This is what the besieged saw from the walls. In smoke and fire the great host, as Byron's well-known poem pictured it, rolled on to Jerusalem. Like Priam, in Homer's Iliad, viewing with Helen the chiefs of the Greeks from the ramparts of Troy, the folk of Jerusalem had watched the Assyrian princes, had heard the taunting Rabshakeh's voice from their fortifications. Screening Jerusalem, the army had gone south, to its visitation of plague and death. Like some surf-shattered wreck of a great ocean-going galley, a great achievement of man's hands, helpless and breaking on the beach, the armoured host had fallen.

**9–11** Relief, the fear gone, and fear it was, when the prospect was the merciless victory of the most cruel nation that evil had so far spawned upon the earth, peace for horror – how else could such a gift express itself save in such a cry of joy?

**12–14** The people went out, knew the happiness of opened gates, viewed the walls from the outside, walls undamaged and unbreached, walls that had served them well and blocked out the fierce foe, how beautiful seemed the towers, how graceful the ramparts set into the city's hills. Here was a tale to tell, history made to be turned into song for those yet to be.

Could v. 14 be a better conclusion? The ripe fruit of deliverance is not only joy but confidence, faith renewed and deeper committal.

**Read Psalm 49; Luke 12.16–20; 16.19–31**

### Occasion and author

There is nothing to be said of either. The solemnity of death can be traced through all literature from the Babylonian epic of Gilgamesh to Housman's *Shropshire Lad*. It is a theme in Greek drama, in Lucretius' didactic poem, in the Odes of Horace. It emerges 'in the midst of life', as the burial service puts it. De Quincey confessed to an obsession with death on any summer's day. The index of the Oxford Dictionary of Quotations has six columns of references to death. The psalm, therefore, needs no special occasion. It might at any time have surged up in a poet's consciousness, the solemnity of a rich sinner's passing, the brash confidence of a living villain, the pathos of the early death of the good and godly – a thousand different situations which throng the days of our lives.

**Commentary**

**1–4** Perhaps the psalm is placed here in the collection because it is directed to mankind. Like the altogether different hymn which precedes, this poem has the world for its audience, for all men living are subject to death. He proclaims, like any writer of 'wisdom literature' that he has deep truths to set to poetry and music (4), a message of import to be heard. No hint of time or dating is contained in such an introduction. Wisdom is as old as the reflective mind of man, its expression as ancient as the techniques of ordered speech. R. K. Harrison puts it well: 'I will clothe my thoughts in proverbial form. With the twang of a harp I will solve my problem'.

**5–14** The sombre theme reminds the reader of Ecclesiastes, and the parables of the Rich Fool and the Rich Man and Lazarus. Or it might be A. E. Housman translating an ode of Horace (4.7):

*But oh, whate'er the sky-led seasons mar,*
*Moon upon moon rebuilds it with her beams.*
*Come we where Tullus and where Ancus are,*
*And good Aeneas, we are dust and dreams . . .*

'Truly no man can ransom himself, or give to God the price of his life, for the ransom of his life is costly, and can never suffice, that he should continue to live on for ever, and never see the Pit' (7–9, RSV).

It is 'the old wind in the old anger', as the same Housman said. Here is a voice from the dawn of literature: 'Gilgamesh spake unto Utnapishti, the Far Distant . . . How could my cheeks be not wasted, not sunken my face, my mind not distraught and my countenance not fallen? . . . for my friend, even Enkidu, we who stood together . . . Oh, my friend whom I so dearly loved, who walked beside me through all adventures – him has the fate of mankind overtaken.'

Nothing avails. Neither wealth nor wisdom avert the common doom. 'The paths of glory lead but to the grave.' Death shepherds his helpless flock into the grave (14). They leave all behind them, for there are no pockets in a shroud (10).

**15** So far the theme might be the common poetry of man faced with the Last Enemy, but the beginning of a new hope begins to emerge in v. 14. The good and the bad are not the same in that final hour, a startling thought in that ancient context which this verse carries to an equally startling conclusion. It has been too rashly alleged that the Old Testament knew nothing of a wider hope. The final verb is the same as that used of Enoch's strange passing (Gen. 5.24). Nothing, the writer quite obviously believed, even the last grim experience, can separate man from the love of God. It might appear that the man who wrote this psalm was haunted by the abrupt and cryptic phrase about Enoch. With like staccato style he poured his faith into this one sharp phrase – faith indeed, for he knew no empty tomb or risen Lord. He merely knew that God was good, and a like ending for arrogant and unrepentant evil seemed illogical.

**16–20** The psalm ends with the same conclusion as Psa. 37. There is a redressing of the balance, a final reckoning, a vindication of justice. Otherwise the world would indeed be 'darkness to the core'. The ruthless rich may get from life what he seeks to get. People often do. But what do they seek? Barns rebuilt and stuffed again? And the end is by no means fixed, as the fool of the Lord's small story found. The term of enjoyment is based on no Faustian bargain. No one controls but God.

In the closing verse the KJV is to be preferred to the versions which reject 'and understandeth not'. It is the insight into life's true values, comprehension of the theme which the psalm has sought to develop, that makes a person human.

**Conclusion**

It is therefore calmness (16) before the vast confusion of life, the brevity which seems at times to obscure the final consummation of a mighty plan, which the psalmist counsels. If this life is not all, then all is well – and only then. Otherwise, as we have quoted the sombre Housman:

> *'twere iniquity on high*
> *To cheat our sentenced souls of aught they crave*
> *And mar the merriment as you and I*
> *Fare on our long fool's errand to the grave.*

And imagine how long such 'merriment' and the society based upon it, would endure.

**Read Psalm 50; Isaiah 1**

**Occasion and author**

Asaph is set down as the writer of this psalm. This man, a descendant of Gershom, seems to have held some role as a master of music in David's day. He was, however, also looked upon as the originator of a guild, 'the sons of Asaph', which continued to the days of the Restoration. In consequence, any particular poem need not be attributed to the original singer. It could possibly be from his school. Any dictionary of the Bible or concordance will supply the exhaustive list of references. This piece, a stern polemic about formalism in worship or inadequate ideas of God, reads like a page from Isaiah – and not only Isaiah, for scorn poured on meaningless ritual and sacrifice was a constant prophetic theme (Amos 5.21–26; Hos. 6.6; 8.13; Mic. 6.6–8; Jer. 7.21–23). Some place the psalm in the days of Hezekiah's revival.

**Commentary**

**1–6** Perhaps the psalm is placed here because it appears to be addressed to humanity at large, an emerging theme in adjacent psalms. The picture is Zion as another Sinai, with God blazing forth in glory to rebuke worship that contained no reality. From east to west, like the travelling sun, God's glory flares, challenging to true worship. Suddenly, with vs. 4 and 5, the beam turns blindingly on Israel. She, too, is on trial, and with less excuse for her guilt than the heathen of the world.

**7–15** 'Hear, O Israel . . .' ran the Shema (Deut. 6.4,5), and no Israelite could fail to start to attention at the words 'hear, and I will testify against you.' They are no longer spectators but the arraigned. Judgement is beginning where it must begin, with 'the household of God'. The mere performance of ritual, the sacrifice of a beast, the doling out of tithes, do no more than degrade God to the level of a heathen deity. The Babylonian epic of Gilgamesh pictures the celestial ones clustering over the ascending smell of burnt offerings and finding their pleasure in them. It is what an act means that matters. No man can buy God's favour with gift or sacrifice. The Pharisee in the Lord's story, mouthing his boasts of formal piety, makes a ludicrous figure. It was the despised official, in agony over his sin, who 'went down to his house justified'. It is gratitude which enlivens and makes real the worship (14).

**16–23** Thus far the dull and ignorant are dealt with. Their sin is crass carnality and a low view of God. Any line of theological thought which ends in a distorted, bent or repellent conception of God must necessarily be wrong, and it is of small use for those persisting in such error to hide behind baseless definitions of corrupt human reasoning or inexplicable acts of divine 'sovereignty'. Man must understand. The last verse of the preceding psalm insisted on this human characteristic – indeed, man's one demarcation from the brute. This prophetic psalm insists that sacrifice and offering had value only in so far as they signified something far greater. Such folk were foolish, reprehensibly foolish, but stand in a category different from the wicked addressed in the last six verses of the psalm, the hypocrites, the rebels, and the self-willed transgressors of the Decalogue (17–20). God has withheld His hand. He has seemed, as He so often seems, to do nothing. The sinners, prospering like those in view in the preceding psalm, think that God does not act, because, like them, He condones evil. They reverse truth and make God in their image, a common and hideous fault of man. Their convenient god was 'permissive' – 'he's a good fellow and 'twill all be well', as Omar Khayyam makes his pot say in the satire of the Potter's Shop.

Judgement ultimately comes (22) and righteousness is at last vindicated. Life is sometimes too short a span for a man to see and know this truth from personal experience, but many an experienced Christian lives long enough to outlive 'the green bay tree'. If not, he 'shall know hereafter'.

**Conclusion**

Let it be in the words of Professor J. J. S. Perowne: 'The instruction of the psalm abides: it has not lost its force. The sacraments and ordinances of the Christian Church may become to us what sacrifice and offering became to some Jews; a man may give all his goods to feed the poor and yet have no love; a man may be punctual in his attendance at all holy ordinances, and yet cherish iniquity in his heart, and upon occasion, secretly practise it. Hence the psalm is truly prophetical; that is, universal in its character. It deals with "the sinners and the hypocrites in Zion", but it reaches to all men, in all places to the end of time.'

# 51

**Read Psalm 51; 2 Samuel 11.2–12.14**

## Occasion and author

It is painful to find commentators who would deny the Davidic authorship of this most moving of the penitential psalms, painful because it is principally in the study of the Bible that this dogged obstinacy to deny tradition, to murder by dissection, and to destroy spiritual value, are found. It is difficult for one whose literary training is in another branch of ancient literature to view such subjective comment with other than impatience. A group of Davidic psalms begins here, and fills most of the remainder of Book Two. The link is with 50.7–14. Verses 16 and 17 of this psalm of a sinner's agony pick up that prophetic thought, and provide the link which the rabbinical editors seem to have found attractive in placing the psalms. Then, having turned again to a psalm of the Davidic Psalter, they continued for some score of poems. The last two verses, where the psalm becomes general, may be a later addition. They seem to reflect a time when the walls of Jerusalem lay in ruin. This seems to point to the Exile, during which time the repentance of David was taken up by a penitent nation, and his psalm made the vehicle of a people's contrition. This suggestion in no way takes from the value of the psalm, or diminishes the divine authority of the ending.

The circumstances of David's appalling sin are well enough known. In the comfort of the city, amid the adulation of an eastern court, the great psalmist's heart had grown cold. None rebuked him. His power was absolute, and corrupted him. What part in the lamentable incident Bathsheba played is not clear to see. What, after all, was she about, in her husband's absence, thus to be exposed to view? She is not blamed, but it is difficult not to believe that her blame was great. She was a subtle, clever woman and was too easy a conquest to be acquitted of a part in the adultery and the murder which fill the shameful story. Two figures only stand out – the manly soldier, Uriah, a convert from the Hittite race, and brave Nathan, who saw what had to be done, and at peril of his life did it, breaking, with a courageous sentence the shell of insensitive and unfeeling self-righteousness which

David wore, and whose wearing shows the sickness of his soul and the distance he had slipped from the God he once had served.

**Commentary**

**1** David knew that he had no claims on God. It was 'mercy all, immense and free'. Only in the exercise of God's 'steadfast love', as the RSV puts it, unnecessarily changing the beautiful word 'loving-kindness', could he find relief. Casting himself on God's grace, God's unmerited love, he asks that his sins be wiped out. It is possible to wash the ink (composed, perhaps, of soot and glue) from a pumice-smoothed papyrus. Thus a debt is cancelled. Compare similar contexts of metaphor – the blotting out of Moses's name, for example (Exod. 32.32), or the ritual cancellation of Num. 5.23. Paul picks it up in Col. 2.14.

**2** The metaphor continues. Aware, at last, of the pathetic creature, too long hidden beneath the incongruous trappings of royalty, David feels soiled in person, contaminated to the depths, in a fashion which needs washing, washing, washing – cleansing. He lays hold of words to express his need, and to be rid of a clinging, soiling thing, but finds the verbs inadequate.

**3** His sin is an obsession, an incubus, standing like a presence before his eyes. It is 'never out of his mind' (Moffatt). It 'confronts him continually' (Harrison). How true is the experience, too many thousands know. It was the more obsessive because of the long months of numbed conscience over the whole evil situation.

**4** All in fact, had seemed secure. It was not by any means hidden. David had betrayed himself into the hands of the murderous Joab, and was to learn that he could no longer discipline that turbulent man. He was demeaned before his own family, and was to pay a price for that. Above all, he had forgotten the God he once had known so well. He had betrayed his Lord. He had committed crimes against a woman, her gallant husband, his base accomplice, his polluted family, the nation which trusted him, the Levites who sang his songs – crimes, yes, but against the now real and looming presence of the forgotten Lord of half-forgotten days, it was sin, evil done under His watching eye. The result? Yes, result, because the Hebrew mind did not distinguish between consequence and purpose, the result was vindication of the words of God – 'Be sure your sin will find you out', 'The soul that sins it shall die', 'You shall not kill . . . commit adultery . . . covet your neighbour's wife' – a thousand words came hammering, battering upon his brain.

**5** O God, how to be free and whole, when the roots of it all, as he now could see, went back to the beginning of being?

**6** Sin was, and is, rooted in self-deception, bedded in the core of the personality. The whole ghastly tale did not begin with illicit staring from the palace roof at a woman probably too willingly exhibited. A hundred unseen surrenders, tolerated lust, had prepared the way and sapped the defences. Sin begins in the mind, in the depths of a corrupted heart and it is there, in the secret place, that the remedy must begin.

**7** Purge, cleanse, purify, wash – the awful need for emancipation grips and tears him. 'So wash me thou, without, within,' he seems to cry, 'purge me with fire if that must be.' The switch made of hyssop was used to sprinkle the symbolic blood in the ritual of cleansing prescribed in the Levitical law. Hence the metaphor . . . Sprinkle the blood, do anything!

**8** Misery becomes unbearable, and the spirit longs for the joy it took for granted, and the gladness of happier days wantonly thrown away.

**9** And that can only be if the steady, accusing gaze of God can turn away. 'The Lord turned and looked at Peter . . . And he went out and wept bitterly.' If God could only hide His face, His saddened face.

**10** Helpless, helpless, helpless. If God turns away, even if He wipes out the sin, the evil propensity, the bend in the heart, the stain within still remains. That is how, that is why, in the intensity of his desire, David breaks through to Christ's own solution. 'You must be born again' – or to Ezekiel's deep insight: 'A new heart I will give you, and a new spirit I will put within you . . .' (Ezek. 36.25–27).

**11** He does not want God to hide His face, any more than Peter in the boat, overwhelmed by the reality of Christ, really wanted the Lord to depart (Luke 5.8). He was hungry now for the blessed presence of God, for the buoyancy of the Holy Spirit sustaining his heart, infusing his resolution, uplifting, fortifying.

**12** He was thirsty for the joy he once had known in those glad, free days before the weight of royalty bore down upon his spirit, under the stars at Bethlehem, out in the Judean wilderness, when Saul pursued, when, indwelt by the emancipating Spirit of his God, he had outrun a host and laughed at peril.

**13** How otherwise could he tell others of his God? How, one might well wonder, with a record so soiled, a testimony so scorned? It is well to remember that this was a hymn written to be publicly sung. The Levites were to sing in antiphonal chorus these very words of fierce sincerity and ruthless self-exposure, before any congregation which chose to gather to hear the voice of their king's contrition. Could any confession be more agonizingly complete? Is there any better way to 'teach sinners' God's ways, and convert those who will listen to their God? David flung his person in the path of the tempted to turn them back from sin.

**14** The psalm has reached a climax with v. 13. In quiet tones he now utters the more formal words of a sinner's petition.

**15** He gives his power of song, used to such self-wounding purpose, to God to use. Can there be better sacrifice?

**16** Can there, indeed? Bullocks and the fat of lambs, what could these trifles mean to the wealthiest man in Israel?

**17** He had given far more, a broken spirit and a wounded heart. 'You will not scorn a broken and penitent heart, O God', as R. K. Harrison simply translates it.

**18,19** We have suggested that a tormented Israel, equally conscious of the treason of its sin, added these verses to the psalm, to appropriate its language to themselves. It is intensely moving to see such public action. Could our own nation rise to it?

**Conclusion**

Could we individually rise to such identification? We dismissed 'penance', and with true repentance no penance is prescribed. But could any man, rescued from grievous sin, and at Christ's cost redeemed, forgiven, restored, do better than mark the solemn occasion by learning as a prayer, learning by heart, the first seventeen verses of this penitential psalm?

**Read Psalm 52; 1 Samuel 21.7–9; 22.6–23**

### Occasion and author

Rabbinical tradition, not to be despised, assigns this psalm to the traumatic experience with the base Doeg. It is a loathsome thing to have treachery slide, serpent-fashion across the path. The spirit revolts, and it was David's way to empty the pollution out into passionate poetry, interfused with prayer. Hence this poem.

### Commentary

**1–7** Doeg, as the title informs us, was the 'mighty man'. He was Saul's herdsman and had informed the mad king that Ahimelech, priest of Nob, had supplied David with some provisions. Guerrilla groups can survive only by the goodwill and clandestine help of the local population, and it is the common fashion of those who seek to suppress such insurgency to deal savagely with the population which gives them aid and comfort. Saul's massacre at Nob was a crime which can be paralleled up to Lidice and My Lai. David, as the story makes clear, was horrified at the ruin which he had unwittingly brought upon an innocent community. The blistering words of the psalm were the weapon David used against the evil executor of Saul's evil and cruelty. There is no doubt that, in the context of the Hebrew religion, they would weigh with devastating strength on the man who had done the deed. A curse was a terrible thing to the ancient Eastern mind, as it is still to the desert Bedouin. Safe from David's sword, Doeg was not safe from his pen and such words could destroy him.
**8,9** As though to cleanse his mind and lips of the violence they had shaped, David closes the psalm with a promise and an aspiration. Perhaps an olive grew in the courtyard of the shrine of devastated Nob. It is a rich image.

The olive was life to the ancient Eastern world. Indeed, even today the economy of some of its lands would stagger if the precious tree failed. The traveller finds it everywhere. It grows grey-green on the slopes of Tivoli looking across the wide plain towards the far smoke of Rome, colouring the hills with its pastel hues as uniformly as it did when Tivoli was Tibur and Hadrian built his vast villa on the levels below.

It grows hungrily on Corfu, clustering on the narrow neck of land at Palaeokastritsa, where Alcinous entertained the hero Odysseus in one of the most colourful tales of Homer's epic of wandering and adventure.

From Delphi the visitor looks down from the heights above the deep valley and sees the Amphissian Plain – one meandering and widening olive-grove running like a dark stream of lava to the far Corinthian gulf, where the port of Itea strings a line of white dots against the blue.

The serried groves of Lebanon, the scattered trees on the Galilee hills above the azure of the lake, gnarled and incredibly old in the Garden of Gethsemane . . . the stocky, sturdy tree is everywhere.

It is the living symbol of indestructible vitality. It grows best in what most trees would find a hostile environment. In the fertile valleys, to be sure, the fruit will grow large and round, but there is more oil in the fruit from the harsh and stony slopes, where a good tree will produce half a ton of oil a year. Nothing can kill the olive.

In Athens the citizens were so conscious of their dependence on the olive that they had a law which forbade the grubbing out of apparently dead and ravaged stumps. Such stumps were fenced and inspected annually, and dire penalties attended any circumvention of the law. A speech of the great orator Lysias survives in which an alleged offender defends himself in court against such a charge. Hence the awe with which the visitor looks on the few huge-boled and twisted trunks of the surviving olives of Gethsemane.

A large public garden once ran up the slopes of the Mount of Olives. Most of the area has been covered by the crude invasion of church and basilica, with rival cults anxious to crowd the sacred spot. The Romans destroyed the whole grove along with the city across the nearby Kedron. But were all the old stumps utterly destroyed? The centuries seem tangled in the torn and twisted wood, and it is not at all impossible that today's trees draw sustenance from roots which gripped the stony soil beneath the knees of Christ.

If the psalmist's image is pressed to its conclusions, there is great encouragement here for Christians. They, too, bring essential life to a world which might perish without them. They, too, produce their finest quality when conditions are harsh, and little else will grow. Nor let them despair of the damaged, battered stump, cut by the enemy, and no longer bearing fruit. Let it be walled in and cherished, and if life was ever there it will one day sprout again, sprout with green which will be tender and need fostering care:

*Like the vase in which roses have once been distilled,*
*You may break, you may shatter the vase if you will,*
*But the scent of the roses will cling to it still.*

Protect the backslider and coax him back to fruit-bearing.

'I am a green olive in the temple of God.' When the Persians over-ran Athens and burned bare the mighty rock platform of the Acropolis, Athena's olive was blasted by the flames. The Persians withdrew, battered to retreat by Greek ships and Greek valour, and, returning to their ruined city, the Athenians found the olive on the hill putting out fresh green shoots.

They set to work and put together new buildings at whose shattered remnants the world still wonders. They produced half a century of such achievement in art, architecture, literature and thought, as the world had never seen, and has not seen since. The verve, passion, enthusiasm which sprang from their great triumph over Asia and its peril, was turned into energy, creativity and a vivid life which marked all history for good. The olive sprouting by the shrine was the first hint of the mighty hope which held and changed and rejuvenated a people, and led them to change all man's story.

If Christian men, 'olives in God's temple', can seize the thought, and translate into living activity all the wealth of meaning which lies in the psalmist's picture of the strong, vital, valiant, rich, sturdy and enduring tree, such a renaissance might yet come to the Church and to society.

**Read Psalms 14; 53**

**Occasion and author**

This is a second version of Psalm Fourteen, save for a few details. As with the psalms of the Second Book, the name Elohim is used for God instead of Jehovah – or Yahweh, as the more accurate, but less time-honoured transliteration of the appellation is. In vs. 5 and 6 the language varies from the earlier version. Perhaps the changed words were designed to meet a new situation of peril. Was it used, with small adaptations, in the days of the Assyrian Terror, and preserved as a memorial of an old Davidic hymn, which served well a fear-ridden populace in a day of grim menace? There must have been some compelling reason for the reproduction of a revered psalm with what seems, for want of knowledge, to be arbitrary alteration. Speculation is fruitless. There is something that is not known, a fine field of guesswork but a source of little profit. Look back at the comments on Psa. 14.

**Read Psalm 54; 1 Samuel 23**

## Occasion and author

To be betrayed by a villain like Doeg was damaging enough to a person like David who loathed lies and treachery. To find disloyalty and treason among his own people was an experience even more bitter and cruel. He was rejected by his own tribesmen in spite of his rescue of one of their own exposed frontier settlements from a Philistine inroad. They were not 'strangers' who had turned on him but 'insolent men', as the RSV correctly has it. The circumstances are clear enough in the record. David's band was six hundred strong and they had taken refuge in Keilah, which he rescued from a Philistine attack. It was base ingratitude that the townsfolk were not prepared to protect him from his enemy, Saul.

## Commentary

**1,2** 'Save me, O God, because you are a Saviour', is the virtual meaning of the phrase. 'By thy name' means 'because you are what you are'. 'Vindicate me by thy might,' says the RSV. David had committed his cause to God's protection and longed for the visible manifestation of the Lord's approval.
**3** The 'insolent men' and the 'oppressors' were the townsfolk. They were realists rather than ingrates, though the two went together. They had survived the attack of the alien. They were in no mood for a siege by Saul.
**4–7** Such was the situation, desperate enough. David had God alone, but that, he decides, in a surge of faith, is all that is necessary. The principle stands firm – evil is suicidal (5). Secondly, God is good (6). Finally, the God who helped in the past will equally help in the future (7).

## Conclusion

It is a tiny model of a prayer in days of assault and persecution. Prayers need not be long. Consider Sir Jacob Astley before the Battle of Edgehill: 'O Lord! Thou knowest how busy I must be this day. If I forget Thee, do not Thou forget me.'

**Read Psalm 55; 2 Samuel 15.31**

**Occasion and author**

As Maclaren solemnly remarks, the claim that David wrote this psalm has at least as much to say for it as other conjectures. It might be added that the ancient ascription at least constitutes an overwhelming argument. The Absalom rebellion, the betrayals, the base treacheries and the retreat from the city are a likely background. Perhaps Ahithophel was the traitorous friend. It has been suggested that Ahithophel was a relative of Bathsheba but there is no evidence for this. There are few psalms more painful.

**Commentary**

**1,2** The psalmist is overwhelmed with a sense of abandonment. Why has God permitted this? 'Hide not thyself' is an expression used in the humane command of Deut. 22.1–4 for the callous ignoring of another's trouble. If God could so direct in the common patterns of human deprivation, how much more should He regard the plea of one so desolate as an exiled king! 'I am overcome,' says v. 2 as the RSV renders it ('I cannot rest for complaining', says the JB). It is a prayer to be forgiven for too passionate praying. The reason is given in the final phrase 'I am distraught,' and in the extremities of life an old habit had risen to the surface of the mind – David turned to God. The whole grim experience had been permitted to this end.

**3** Here is the cause. A group had cohered, unseen, unsuspected. Part of David's trouble was that he had been screened from reality. Mind suddenly awake, agonizingly aware of what he should long since have seen, he realizes that those he thought were subjects, puppets, mere figures round the court, were alive with hate and not without formidable power. 'They bring misery crashing down on me,' says the JB. There is more than the 'noise' of an enemy. It is 'shrill clamour', the yell of a pursuing pack, 'foemen leaning on his shield', as Alfred puts it in Chesterton's poem, 'and roaring on him when he reeled.'

**4,5** The reaction was violent. 'My heart is awhirl inside me. Deadly terror has engulfed me. Fear and trembling overtake me and shivering seizes me.' The word rendered 'horror' in the KJV is found only in three other contexts – Job 21.6, Isa. 21.4, Ezek. 7.18 – grim contexts all which speak of the dark night of the soul. It is possible that this psalm could be placed in time just before the retreat and the emerging situation which runs from

Psa. 3 to Psa. 6. David is still in the city, almost paralysed with shock, so sudden was Absalom's attack.

**6,7** Hence the thought of retreat so competently carried out when the old fighting-man regained his composure. The first thought is escape. It was Israel's old instinct to seek the wilderness. David, as we saw, was moved to fall back on the old lands of his brave days, the people of his past, the bases of his strength. The first thought was mere escape from the fetid atmosphere of treacherous Jerusalem. The creative and constructive sequel was to come later. Withdrawal, as the Toynbee doctrine has it, leads to Return.

**8** So fled Elijah, so fled Moses, escaping to come back. It is sometimes the only way. Dunkirk leads to D Day.

**9–11** Cities began with Cain. Babylon, Nineveh and Rome are biblical symbols of evil. This century, more than any other since the first, can appreciate how truly the city can become the habitation of every form of human evil. The city had betrayed David. He now knew what the unseen denizens of slum and palace meant. The words could apply today. The vast and arrogant symbols of man's Babel-ridden ways are to be seen in every land.

**12–14** And the city, unkindest cut of all, had corrupted one once trusted, once named a friend, once a sharer in worship and devotion, and now unmasked to reveal the foul face and darkened heart beneath. David holds back from the more awful words he might have said, for he had said all in Psa. 51, but could he speak thus without seeing Nathan's pointing finger and remembering a friend named Uriah (2 Sam. 23.39) to whom he had done such evil as had now been done to him?

**15** As though to wrench himself from a thought so agonizing, in a fire of indignation he calls down judgement on those who had spawned the hour's evil. Perhaps to see himself as another Moses, betrayed by another Korah, gave some relief from the crushing burden of personal reproach (Num. 16.30). So ends the second strophe of the poem.

**16–19** Driven at last to quieter prayer, perhaps thanks to the habits of quieter days (evening, morning, noon), the tormented suppliant seems to find peace. In the psalms of the retreat (3,4,5,6,23) we seemed to distinguish such a pattern of devotion. Prayer can become formal, but even so establish a habit, and that habit can bring peace when the mind is too numb with dire catastrophe to think coherently. The section seems to end in peace.

**20–23** But not without a final struggle with pain. The traitor, the man with what the Germans call 'butterwords', still haunts the memory. 'Glatt sind die Butterlippen seines Mundes', translates Ewald. 'Smooth are his mouth's buttered lips.'

**Conclusion**

What better lesson is there than v. 22 which Peter passed on (1 Pet. 5.7). It had been difficult to do so in the hour of such cascading misery, but the triumph was won. 'Cast your burden on the Lord.' He had achieved the impossible – by retreat to the wilderness, clean, lonely, the scene of old blessedness. 'Unload your burden . . . he will support you.' So simple, but to reach that point can be a Dolorous Way.

# 56

## Read Psalm 56

### Occasion and author

Was this the shameful occasion of David's desperate defection to the Philistine foe? Or was there an unrecorded misfortune in which David fell prisoner and was taken to the town of Goliath, his old enemy of the Elah valley? The latter seems more likely. The record is brief and there may be much untold. Perhaps the stories of 1 Sam. 21 and 22 telescope. David 'escaped', says 22.1, to his old refuge of Adullam. A tract of the story of the precarious sojourn in the Philistine plain may have been omitted. The psalm is placed here because it is another poem of distress.

### Commentary

**1,2** Lonely battle, and a sense of an opposing multitude (Psa. 3) are a common enough experience in life . . . 'many of them are fighting me bitterly,' Harrison renders. They 'pant' after him (1) as if in vicious pursuit. The malice of men against those they hate justifies too often both metaphors. It is the word of Job 5.5 where the RSV renders the last phrase 'the thirsty pant after his wealth', breathing heavily, as it were, with fierce desire.

**3** A fine verse, bravely said. Then is the time to trust, and surely those commentators who see a psychological contradiction in the verse have been fortunate in their dreams of peace. There is no need to explain to most people who have confronted the direr deeds of life that fear is faith's testing. It is a blessed habit to acquire, the turning from a menace which stands before to the trust which looks up and beyond it.

**4** The verse forms the psalm's refrain (10,11; 118.6; Heb. 13.6). To commit such determination to a form of words, a liturgy, if you will, is a salutary spur to bravery. There are times when thought is overwhelmed and quiet reason paralysed. Courage becomes automatic at such times if courage has been committed to habit and encased in a form of words on lesser occasions. Hence the benefit of learning Scripture by heart.

**5** The attack is unremitting, slanderous. 'Words' in Hebrew can mean 'circumstances', and the meaning can be that a determined foe can take every detail of life, twist, bend and pervert it to harm. The foe is inventive, deceptive, a treacherous creature like his 'father the devil whose desires he does'.

**6** 'My heels', literally. The organized evil is close behind snapping at the exposed heels, like the serpent of Gen. 3.15. The ambush is more commonly evil's method than the frontal assault (Luke 11.53,54). The Philistines' reason for this attack on the mind of their prisoner is difficult to grasp. Why not physical elimination? The notable refugee was in their hands, and some fierce struggle to resist, some diabolical programme of harassment, is reflected in the prayer.

**7** Hence the vehemence of the distracted man, and his ire against his persecutors.

**8** Hence, too, his sole hope. He has wandered (KJV), but God knows where. The RSV has no reason to abandon the word, though the singular of the original ('my wandering') might have been effectively kept. He observes the fall of the sparrow. He knows the weary way. 'The raven he feedeth, so why should I fear . . .?'

**9–12** The refrain is repeated perhaps with a stronger note of certainty. Calvin comments: 'Though God may have seemed to depart from me . . . still will I rest in His word . . . Though God furnishes believers with manifold subjects of praise . . . still they can scarcely take three steps unless they have learned to lean only on the word.'

**13** Let us keep the KJV's rendering in this final verse as a conclusion to the prayer. It so eminently fits the experience of the Christian each and every day. The great step is made. The soul is redeemed. The transaction is done. The daily walk remains and in each day's firm walking the watching world sees the worth and the reality of the transforming grace. The Christian is the world's most legible gospel – and 'what if the print be crooked, what if the type be blurred?'

**Read Psalm 57; Deuteronomy 32.1–14**

**Occasion and author**

The ancient title says that the psalm was written by David 'when he fled from Saul into the cave' ('into' is the Septuagint rendering). Was the escape rather from Gath, and the compromising or perilous situation which inspired the preceding psalm? The actual text gives no clue on the precise occasion, nor makes it clear whether the cave was David's old refuge of Adullam or one of the many caves along the shores of the Dead Sea in the wadis of the eastern Judean wilderness from Engedi to Qumran. The former hiding place was closer to the Philistine plain and the westward valleys of the uplands. Nothing certain can be said.

**Commentary**

**1–3** The psalm opens, like its predecessor, with a plea for God's mercy. The rocky refuge suggests the first word picture, the beautiful figure of Deut. 32.11, one varied and elaborated by the tender words of Christ Himself (Matt. 23.37). The whole concept of God's tenderness is characteristic of the Old Testament and sets the Hebrew faith far apart from the notions of surrounding paganism with demonic deities and monstrous reflections of base humanity. The change of tense in the first verse has significance. The psalmist looks back to the past and on to the future. Experience fortifies hope, and the emergence of this thought determines the shape of the next two verses. The storm of destruction rages down the valley of life. It will pass as such tumults pass, and Elijah's 'voice of silence' will follow. As God has saved, so will He save from those that 'pant for his life'. It is the verb of 56.1 and 2. John De Witt's rendering suggests: 'He will send from heaven to save me from the revilers that pant for my life'. It is a difficult expression to render, and both RSV and Moffatt decide for 'trample on me'. Both metaphors suggest close and perilous pursuit, stayed from its objective only by God. Kidner suggests, 'Those who hotly pursue me', and points to the enlargement of the figure which follows. It is easy to see why the editors placed these two psalms of retreat together.

**4,5** A tumbled and vivid picture of dire danger. Part of the unknown circumstances behind these two psalms is some assault of the tongue, a type of attack which David always found it most difficult to endure. The refrain, which appears again at the end of the psalm, suggests that the psalmist's remedy from entangling evil was to look up to God's heavenly majesty.

Men 'that are set on fire' is rendered simply 'man-eaters' by the NEB, a translation consistent with 'lions'.

**6** Perhaps this verse rather than the next should be taken as the turning point and the second movement of the psalm. One might imagine that the poem represents a sudden change of fortune, even that this verse to the end was written later than the first five verses. The pursuit is not only checked; there is a reversal of fortune. Their own pit has swallowed them. Their plans of death have recoiled.

**7–11** Perhaps 'I will awake the dawn' (8) is an indication that it was night which brought defeat and confusion to some hot pursuit, and courage to the fugitive. The glow of light is over the mauve Moab uplands. All is quiet in the ravine. The still air carries no sound of war. Hence the outburst of jubilation, rapidly and nobly transformed (9) into a desire to proclaim the goodness of God, and an equally consuming passion of praise (10). Few passages in the Psalter more truly catch the true spirit of worship than these verses.

### Conclusion

It is true that 'sometimes a light surprises . . .' The fetid air of the pagan city is forgotten in the clean, sharp beauty of the dawn in the high hills, the air still damp with the pure dews of night and carrying the scent of every upland flower. Who shall say that it is not good to escape at times and breathe deep of sweeter air?

## 58

**Read Psalm 58; James 5.1–11**

### Occasion and author

Accepting the tradition of Davidic authorship for want of a convincing alternative, it is difficult to fix a time in the record of the psalmist's life when this protest against injustice and tyranny could have been written. It was probably placed here because it accords with the psalms of trouble and trial gathered in this portion of the Psalter. Saul was judge as well as king. Rulers gather their like about them. Injustice and cruelty on the throne finds reflection on the judge's bench. It is common enough to discover in human experience that the faults of leaders multiply beneath them. Faced with the problem of placing a passionate poem of protest, and following some clues of vigorous metaphor ('lions', for example of v. 6 and the 'arrows' of v. 7 – compare 57.4) it seemed appropriate to set the psalm in this place.

**Commentary**

**1** A challenge opens the psalm. Harrison translates: 'Do you indeed decree justice, you sovereign rulers?' The Living Bible modernizes: 'Justice? You high and mighty politicians don't even know the meaning of the word.' It is a difficult verse poorly rendered in the KJV. The RSV is unfortunate in using 'gods' for the 'mighty ones' thus castigated.

**2** The RSV renders this simply and forcefully. No conduct, no judgement can come clean and undefiled from a heart where wickedness lurks. We have considered before the biblical conception of 'the heart', that core of the personality where all thought, speech and action, for good or for ill, originate. It is the nucleus of our being and must be always kept for God's own indwelling. A corrupt judge is one whose corruption seeps out or overflows from a central accumulation of evil. Their hands 'deal out' violence (RSV). 'Dole out,' says the Jerusalem Bible; 'weigh out,' says J.J.S. Perowne. The word is ironical. Pretending to hold impartially the scales of justice and give due weight to the good, the corrupt judges dispense violence.

**3** They are bent from birth, says the psalmist, feeling for some doctrine of original sin, liars from the beginning, reprobates who have never been exposed to the straightening, cleansing power of God.

**4,5** Such men are serpents but, like the deadly adder, so garrisoned and armoured against the Spirit of God that, like some venomous snake that no snake-charmer can hypnotize, they go on their poisonous way untamed. The strange art of the snake-charmer was known in Palestine. Perhaps Jeremiah had this passage in mind when he spoke of 'adders which cannot be charmed' (8.17). Ecclesiastes says drily: 'If the snake bite before it is charmed, the snake-charmer loses his fee' (10.11, NEB). All snakes are deaf. The charmer's art lies in the movement of his pipe.

**6–9** With a sudden gust the style changes to the language of commination. Provision is made for such denunciation in the prayer-book, but it is not generally acceptable under the new covenant. But here it is to be remembered that the rightful king of Israel, at a period of his life when he was athirst for justice, had to watch helplessly while corrupt men perverted the courts and twisted righteous administration out of shape. He denounces them in the name of God and good. The second half of v. 7 (KJV) needs retranslating. The RSV says: 'Like grass let them be trodden down and wither.' Verse 9 is another tangled text. The NEB may be nearest to a correct interpretation: 'All unawares, may they be rooted up like a thornbush, like weeds which a man angrily clears away!'

**10** This verse again must be understood in the context of its rhetoric. Revelation, in its fierce denunciation of a blood-drunken Rome, is as strong, but it is easy, speaking from a place of peace, to deprecate the language of those who are suffering the torments of the bitterly wronged and callously persecuted, especially when a deep consciousness of innocence is calling for redress to a tarrying Heaven. Matthew 23, reports Christ's own denunciation of the hypocrites in power, feeding their evil on the lives of the helpless and the innocent. Only those who, like Ezekiel, have 'sat where they sat' have full right to comment on this language of the wronged.

**11** A certain jealousy for God also infuses the language. Is it not a common enough argument of atheism today: 'Why does God tolerate the vast evil of the world?'

**Conclusion**
It is the quieter finale of Psa. 37 which emerges at the end: 'Wait, I say, on the Lord.' Faith can only lay hold of this hope before the madness, the evil, and the injustice that bestride the earth.

**Read Psalm 59; 1 Samuel 19.11–18**

**Occasion and author**
The psalm obviously belongs to the same series, historically connected with the troubles of David under Saul. In tone and language it is also similar to the four psalms which precede. The crisis lived in David's imagination and there is no hint when the words were written. The thought which obtrudes is that the princess Michal deserved better of her husband than she received. It is a mark against the psalmist's character.

**Commentary**
**1–5** It is obvious that the words are applicable to a wider area of trouble than those circumstances of household siege and treachery which the title suggests. This is not to deny the truth of the tradition, merely to remark that the psalmist universalizes it. The escape from Saul's emissaries was a pattern of many perilous years. Saul had collected a vicious band of police as tyrants tend to do. Underlying the whole story, and the words of the psalm itself, is the vague suggestion that neither the tyrant nor his guards were sure of the popular reaction, if hostility towards the people's favourite soldier was too open. Like the Sanhedrin, 'they feared the people'.
**6,7** The denizens of the night, like prowling packs of dogs, 'slaver at the mouth' (so the JB sustaining the metaphor through the two verses). They are unconscious of the watching eye of God. This is the David of Psa. 2. Or did David, if we rightly dated that vigorous psalm, have this passage in mind?
**8–10** This verse (8) with the reference to divine derision, suggests that such was the case. 'O my Strength' (9, RSV and others) is also reminiscent of the early psalms of the Psalter where God is addressed by various abstract names. So also 'God, my Mercy'. The Lord becomes, for a triumphant faith, Strength and Mercy personified.
**11–13** 'Slay them not' is a fearsome beginning to the prayer for judgement. The psalmist would rather see the slower outworking of retribution, lest the

people forget that judgement is real. The words must be read like those of the earlier commination (Psa. 58) in the light of the sin against the nation for whose fortunes the psalmist feels himself responsible.

**14,15** In fact their punishment is to be what they have chosen. 'Let the unjust be unjust still . . .' (Rev. 22.11). They have roamed the streets like a wild dog pack loosed on the innocent by corrupt authority. Let them roam the same streets, a pack of curs still, but hounded by authority no longer corrupt, hungry and unsatisfied. Sin punishes itself. It is an awful fate to repeat, defeated and humbled, what was chosen in the arrogance of apparent triumph.

**16–18** The refrain returns from v. 9 with a new note of gladness. The psalm has comprehended a whole range of experience from defeat to triumph. Perhaps it was so intended, and perhaps there is a clue to the time of writing. Back in the city David sees the old places of his peril, the dark streets through which he slipped in furtive flight. Perhaps he sees with contempt which seeks no summary vengeance the cringing creatures who, under Saul, rode high. Let them live out their lives, scorned, disarmed. And God be praised who gave the dawn (16).

**Read Psalm 60; 2 Samuel 8**

**Occasion and author**

The old claustrophobia of encircled and embattled Israel is in this psalm and in the chapter in the historical record which forms its background. Like Rome thrusting out from her enclave by the Tiber, and reaching the Forth, the Rhine, the Danube, the Euphrates and the Nile in her vain and never-ending quest for a secure and final frontier, so Israel, at last precariously united under David, set out to clear the borderlands. David was the Augustus of his day, seeking walls for the land. The record of the campaigns to the east, the west and the north shows both the peril of Israel and the strength of her enemies. The resemblance to modern Israel's problems is an uncanny illustration of the manner in which geography determines the patterns of history. Taking an ancient oracle as his cue (Josh. 1.4) David saw the Euphrates and the Mediterranean as his coasts and pushed out towards both. Stretched to the utmost reach of his military strength, the king was in the Syrian curve of the Fertile Crescent, when Edom attacked. The Philistines, who seem to have been in decline, were restive in the Gaza coastlands. It was a dangerous situation, not without its dark days and defeats. The fact is, that Edom's counter-attack was, as Wellington said of Waterloo, a 'near run thing'.

It is a fair guess that David weakened his drive to the Euphrates, and contented himself with heavy tribute from the Syrians, in order to detach Joab with a picked force to strike at Edom. The savagery of Joab's subjugation of the eastern foe reflects the panic which must have spread in David's kingdom before the sudden danger which swept across the Jordan in the absence of the king. Fear often prompts fierce reprisal – a fact to be illustrated from Carthage to Hiroshima. That the Edomites were across the Jordan is clear from the reference to the Valley of Salt at the southern end of the Dead Sea. It is one of those places where the landscape can hardly have changed in three thousand years – the pale mauve of the Moab hills to the east, the hard blue of the level sea, the western skyline notched by the ridge of Masada destined for a grim place in later history, the soil dry, sandy, crackling with a film of salt . . .

**Commentary**

**1–3** Joab's column by forced marches has disappeared to the south. David is still shaken by the news of disaster in the rear, news which has poisoned the jubilation of success and spoiled the northern victories. 'Thou hast . . . broken our defences,' says the RSV, and the word used is that of 2 Sam. 5.20 where the metaphor is that of a breaking dawn. The metaphor then changes to that of an earthquake, with shuddering earth and gaping clefts. Verse 3 in this tumult of imagery goes further. The people stagger, as though drunk with the wine of God's confusion. God has 'made them see' (3, 'Thou hast shewed thy people hard things' [KJV]) their utter weakness apart from Him. To 'make to see' is the causative form of the verb 'to see' by which Hebrew expresses the idea of 'show'. It contains a little more of meaning than the less vigorous English translation (compare 91.16). Confidence in military might called for this demonstration. Alert for God's teaching David saw it for the sharp lesson it was.

**4,5** In spite of the familiar words of the old version, it is probable that the RSV contains the true text and translation: 'Thou hast set up a banner for those who fear thee, to rally to it from the bow.' The NEB version, somewhat different, agrees that these verses show the passing of defeat and despair into exultant victory. The arrow storm of attacking bowmen could be a terrible experience, as Crassus' three legions found in 53 B.C., in the very plains where David was fighting, when the Parthians under Surenas fell on the Roman column near Haran – Carrhae as it was then called. The assurance of protection is finding birth in the suppliant's mind.

**6,7** God speaks 'in his sanctuary'. As in 12.5,6 and again in two later psalms (81 and 95), God is shown dramatically breaking in. Perhaps it is a rhetorical device to express a new-born faith, perhaps it reports some oracle of authoritative priest or prophet, sent or uttered to the king in the hour of crisis. Perhaps they are the words of a forgotten ritual (e.g. Deut. 31.10–13) which in Derek Kidner's characteristically felicitous phrase 'came to him new minted in the crisis'. The Lord merely reminded the despairing John of the old Isaian oracles which he knew so well (Luke 7.22) and so it was with David. Succoth (The Tents) was Jacob's first resting place when, the stern testing of Jabbok done, and Esau no longer a terror, he settled with his people. Shechem, on the west of Jordan, was his second stopping point. Gilead and Manasseh stood respectively east of Jordan or straddling the waterway, both outflanking hostile Moab and Edom. Ephraim and Judah similarly embraced the land. It was as though the covenant of occupation was renewed, the old possession confirmed.

**8** The three principal enemies of the south are dismissed, one of no more importance than the basin in which the guest's feet are washed, Edom the slave to whom the master tosses his discarded shoes. The Philistines remind David of one great moment of his life, when Goliath fell with a crash of heavy armour, and from all the long low ridge of hill rose in one wild cry the shout of Israel's triumph.

**9–12** Let God then lead on. Action follows proclamation, the deed the surge of faith. The army moves on.

**Conclusion**

In a day of defeat there are two courses open, to lie down and accept the disaster, or to refuse and fight back. See Mic. 7.8,9 and J. B. Phillips' rendering of Rom. 8.31–39. Failure is not final. There is always a banner to show where the king stands.

**Read Psalm 61**

**Occasion and author**

The editor's task with this psalm was not difficult. As far as the circumstances lead, it may be justly conjectured that the prayer follows its predecessor naturally, refers to the same difficult occasion, and reflects the same mood.

**Commentary**

**1,2** It would seem 'the end of the earth' to one campaigning by the great river. No Israelite army had penetrated further. It was the ultimate frontier mentioned by the old promise and the desert had to be measured in yards, in 'boots, boots, boots, boots, going up and down again', not in the fleet travel of another age. A rock, too, was a benediction when the desert sun beat down and the body craved for the mercy of shade. Or perhaps the image is a citadel, a high refuge and relief from the overwhelming monotony and vastness of the plain, the flat shimmering sand.

**3,4** A shelter, a strong tower, a tent and the covering of mighty wings, was the cry of the harassed soul. He was exposed, half disarmed after the detaching of Joab's flying column, his flanks and rear were bare and the very desert was a wide open menace. His old instinct as a guerrilla fighter was to use the wadis, the hills and crags, the rocky defiles . . . Without the armour of the landscape, its walls and defences which he knew so well, David felt uneasy and in need of a protector. Hence the prayer for protection.

**5** It is possible that the psalm as David first wrote it ended here, and that v. 5 is an addition by the writer when the psalm was handed to 'the Chief Musician' or 'Choirmaster' for use at some public ceremony of thanksgiving when victory was established and the peace of the realm restored.

**6–8** Likewise, it seems probable that these verses were added, either by the king or with the king's permission when the psalm was adapted for public worship. It would be appropriate for a loyal congregation to sing thus in a species of National Anthem, not indeed quite unlike our own. Such adaptation in no way diminishes the authority of the psalm as a part of Scripture, nor subscribes to the extravagances of those commentators on the psalms who see the Psalter widely mutilated by the liturgical additions and modifications of the choirs and music-masters of the temple services.

### Conclusion

'Let me dwell in thy tent for ever' (4). The guest in desert hospitality was absolutely protected. David was in the far desert and the old instincts of the nomad past were alive within him. The host's protection was limited by the host's power to protect, and no human host could claim invincibility. But suppose the host is God? This is the psalm's theme.

**Read Psalm 62; reread Psalm 39**

### Occasion and author

There is little doubt why the compiler of the Psalter placed this psalm here. There is a continuity of spirit and of mood in this poem and its predecessor. Perhaps, too, he saw some purpose, as he drew near the end of Book Two, and remembered afresh how much of the collection came from the storms of David's life, in ending as he had begun. The Psalter opened with the psalms of Absalom's rebellion. Let the second book end, at a very distinct division in the whole collection, with a group of psalms predominantly born of trouble, yet trouble, as before, breaking through to peace, to confidence and praise. He was still aware of the need to vary shadow with sunshine and that is why the closing group of psalms in this book are not without the brighter moods of tranquillity and praise. It could be that he was a little conscious of the fact that his choice and arrangement stressed perhaps a little too much the utterances of pain. And that could be accounted for by his own experience. If the scribe, the rabbi, or whoever it may have been who set the psalms in order, was a survivor from the Exile, then perhaps he chose first the psalms which had meant much to those who remembered and sang them by the waters of Babylon, in the days when the dispossessed had only the Scriptures, perhaps only the Scriptures they held in memory, on which to base their hope.

**Commentary**

**1,2** The psalm begins with a sharp monosyllable – *ak*, an expression of emphasis underlining a truth perceived anew or freshly. A Scotsman might find the word curiously recognizable. It recurs nine times in six verses (1,2, 4,5,6,9). Sometimes the word is used in a restrictive sense and it is difficult to know whether 'surely' or 'only' is the best rendering here. It should be consistent, however, in all these adjacent contexts. Literally the verse runs: 'Surely, towards God, my soul – silence'. The translators feel a need to supply a verb. The NEB renders: 'Truly my heart waits silently for God', and Moffatt rather movingly: 'Leave it all quietly to God, my soul.' The plain Hebrew text, rugged though it may be, does contain the full meaning. Here lies the last reach of faith – peace, not the Epicurean's calm of selfish detachment, nor the Stoic's tight-lipped defiance of adversity, but the quietness of the troubled child conscious of enfolding arms. God, as the verses continue, is not only the source of salvation. He is Himself strength (my rock) and salvation, because it is impossible to think of either word without thinking of the origin of both. The rock, as an image of safe retreat, is a relic of the old days in the desert.

**3,4** Thus fortified, he can turn and address the foes who press upon him. Translators are at variance over the vivid word picture of the bulging wall, slowly giving way before the relentless, slow pressure of the earth behind it. It is probably a wall on a terraced hillside with the earth compacted behind, and swollen with rain or the expanding roots of plants. Some (KJV) take the wall to be the aggressors, others (most versions) more probably to be the victim. There is no attempt to hide the menace. He is near the brink. It was the implacable purpose of some hostile group to bring him down. Hypocrites and liars, they sought to thrust him from the throne, to 'turn his glory into shame' as he put it when in flight from Absalom (4.2).

**5–8** The opening refrain is taken up but with subtle variation. There is visibly a growing confidence as a rush of eager words takes up the theme – rock, salvation, defence, glory, strength, refuge . . . And the timid adverb 'greatly' (cf. v. 2) has disappeared with the doubt which used it. There is no need to change the word 'moved', as do the RSV and NEB. The text uses the same verb as in v. 2, and the repetition is intended. Confidence, in fact, begets the evangelistic note. The prayer becomes exhortation and the king turns to pass his discovery of faith to his people.

**9,10** Trust in God, has been the allegation, not in men nor in the promises of men. Some trust in the masses, the multitude, the proletariat. Some trust in princes and in potentates. Set them, great or small, in the balances against God, and like an insubstantial puff of air they weigh nothing. Nor do 'the earthly things men set their hearts upon'. As Omar continued, they

*Turn ashes or they prosper and anon,*
*Like snow upon the dusty desert's face,*
*Lighting a little hour or two, are gone.*

Wealth, evilly gained or honestly won, is not a foundation on which to build a life. That is why the Lord called the successful farmer in His biting little parable, a fool. He thought a barnful of wheat was a stand-by for his soul.

**11,12** The formula – once, twice – merely suggests 'this is the great, deep lesson of life'. It is 'not by might nor by power, but by my Spirit' that great victory is won. Strength, power (11), justice (12) are to be found, not in men who are transient, insubstantial; not in things, for they are a delusion and a lie. Such blessings can be found only in God. 'Trust in him at all times, O people.'

### Conclusion

The time comes, as the commander Eleazar told the Jews of Masada, as the final attack on the fortress which they had held so well against the might of Rome, was about to be mounted, the time comes, 'to put into practice what has long been determined.' It is the day of desperation which tests the reality of faith. To write, to speak of the soul's trust in God, is always easier than to 'leave it all quietly to Him', when all else fails, and the heavens seem to give no answer or no aid. But such is the confronting challenge.

**Read Psalm 63; reread Psalms 5 and 6**

### Occasion and author

The tradition has it that this was a psalm of the wilderness when David was king. This almost demands the retreat down to the Jordan and beyond, from Absalom's revolt. Perhaps it should be placed somewhere in the later part of the sequence we suggested from Pss. 2 to 6 and on to 23. The way is weary but confidence is returning in strength. It is a most beautiful psalm, commended for daily reading by both Chrysostom and John Donne. 'Early' (KJV) in the first verse has caused it to be used as a morning hymn. Perhaps its most appropriate occasion then might be when the darkness of the night in the Jabbok gorge had passed, and the little column was emerging on to the sunnier uplands beyond the Jordan. Some versions reject the word 'early', but there is no compelling reason to do so.

**Commentary**

**1** It is they who hunger and thirst after righteousness who find satisfaction. David had known for days, known anew what he had known before as a hungry fugitive, the fierce pressure on the mind of deprivation. Hunger and thirst had been real in that desert land. They had stumbled over hot rock, and dry stream beds. The little food a hasty flight could command, was dwindling or gone. The jackal (10) had skulked in the scrub watching the stumbling band.

**2** So David longed for God. The sanctuary lay far behind on the distant mountain ridges of the land where Jerusalem was in the hands of the rebel prince. But God was confined by no walls of shrine or temple. The great arch of heaven was His tent.

**3,4** That is why worship was as easy in the rough wastelands as it was amid the priestly ceremonial of home. The ardent words are a measure of how truly sorrow had washed David, and how trouble had brought heart and mind back to purity and worship.

**5,6** If Psa. 6 held some of the dark depression of the night of anxiety in the ravine, that Valley of Death's Shadow, this gladder poem suggests that during those oppressive hours other thoughts had come to fortify the soul. David was a man of many moods, exalted, cast down, and in each mood was prayer and poem. As anyone who reads with self-understanding must concede, fear and confidence, doubt and faith can cross the mind like the fleeting cloud shadows on a mountain side. Vergil, who understood the mind of man, pictures Aeneas' perplexity:

*On an ocean of troubles tossed without rest,*
*His mind was divided, thoughts this way, now that,*
*So in a bronze basin, a flickering light*
*Darts on the water . . .*

**7,8** God's shadowing wing has been used as a figure of protecting care three times before (17.8; 36.7; 57.1). The eagle floating high with motionless outspread wings was a familiar sight in the wilderness, the very symbol of wide-watching, all-seeing strength (Job 39.27,28). But more. All down the long slope of the wilderness, across and up the Jabbok, One had gone before, fast and urgent, so that it called for all the strength of those who followed to keep up. They had clung close in following but the speeding guide had led them through. Like the Lord, in that last lonely journey up to Jerusalem (Luke 19.28), God had moved swiftly ahead.

**9–11** No pursuit is visible behind. The Jordan and the desert are a wall now which Absalom must cross. The escape was the first movement of victory. Missing the first swift opportunity Absalom had lost all. In vivid prescience David sees the battlefield which has to be. Triumph is to be theirs who swore allegiance, not to rebels, but to God – 'and silence shall fall on the lips that muttered treason' (11, Knox).

**Read Psalm 64; reread Psalm 7**

## Occasion and author

The closing words of the last psalm suggested this place for the denunciation of plotting and slandering traitors, the authors and architects of the king's troubles. Its pattern is the same as some of the psalms of the last decade (52,57,58,59) – a cry to God for vindication, a vivid description of active evil, and a prediction of evil's overthrow.

## Commentary

**1,2** Conspiracy had preceded open revolt. A long and careful campaign of vilification, undetected by David who had grown remote from reality, had prepared the way for open revolt. Victory, he knew, had to go further and deeper than the triumph on the battlefield which had been envisaged in the last psalm. The battle for men's minds could begin only when the armed forces of the prince had been routed, but battle there must be and battle won, if the roots of the land's evil were to be found and cut.

**3–6** The bow was a formidable weapon in ancient times. In the sculptures of the brutal Assyrians, lions are shown shot through with great shafts, their backs broken and hinder quarters dragging with a deep-driven arrow shattering the spine. Yigael Yadin in his great book on the weapons of ancient war collects from archaeological sources illustrations of all types of bow which man's old warlike ingenuity devised. Bitter words and lies, according to the psalmist, flew as swiftly and struck as deeply from the bent taut power of wicked minds. The ambush has been carefully laid, plotted nation-wide. Silently the winged words, cannily aimed, have found their mark, so unswervingly that the concealed plotters see no thwarting for their devices . . .

**7–10** All this, until suddenly the arrow storm of God's reply. The wounders become the wounded in swift retribution. It is as though their own shafts turned back and fell upon them, fell in such clear, clean and obvious retribution that no one could doubt the source of the riposte. David craved for vindication, but he craved for something deeper than that blessing. He longed for the obvious vindication of God Himself, that it might be seen that evil was not rewarded, that plotting wickedness was futile in the end, and that there was a moral law interwoven with the scheme of things.

### Conclusion

This psalm ends the group of prayers and poems on the psalmist's tribulations. They have been utterances of faith and triumph. The weather now clears and brighter words are to fill the rest of the Second Book. Such is life. Clouds pass and sun breaks through. It is not only the dark hours of the soul which make the words of poetry or the theme of human prayer. For which be praise.

## Read Psalm 65

### Occasion and author

But for the inscription which assigns the psalm to David, it would be tempting to think of Isaiah as the writer of this harvest hymn. The glimpses of a global gospel echo so clearly the closing chapter of Israel's most poetic prophet. Normally the line taken in these studies has been to pay deep respect to ancient traditions of authorship and there is nothing in the psalm which could not have been written by David in one of the quieter moods of his composition. His hymns and prayers were not always struck from the anguish of his heart. Some might suggest that a psalm of David had been expanded by Isaiah or a prophet of his school, and, if that were the case, the inspiration and authority of the psalm would not in any way be diminished. There the question must be left. The beauty and the power of the psalm remain.

### Commentary

**1** The first verse appears to be accurately rendered in the older versions. The Alexandrian rabbis turned it into the Greek of the Septuagint in words which simply say: 'a hymn is fitting for Thee'. Literally the words run: 'Praise is silence for Thee', or just possibly: 'Silence is praise'. The notions of waiting and keeping silent are not far apart. Hence the reasonableness of the common translation. Perhaps the picture is the Levite choir poised to sing, awaiting the leader's word.

**2** And the words which follow introduce the song. Prayer is universal. No nation under heaven has lacked some form of prayer.

**3** And universally the first movements of prayer are the confessions of unworthiness. It is part of the beauty and insight of this prayer that confession is followed unhesitatingly by the claiming of forgiveness. Sin, he says, 'has been too strong for me.'

**4** Another beatitude emerges and a verse which almost reaches into the New Testament and to the work of One who 'broke down the middle wall of partition' (Eph. 2.14,15, KJV).

**5** 'Terrible things' ('dread deeds', RSV) are awesome acts. Any answer to prayer should thus stir the soul. Man takes God too readily for granted, too easily makes Him like himself (Psa. 50.21). Nor could Israel forget the 'dread deeds' of the 'outstretched arm' which had brought them out of bondage. Our own standing with God should never fail to be linked in worship and devotion with the event of all events, Christ's death. We write thus, we pray thus, we approach 'boldly' the Eternal Throne, because of the 'dread deed', the awesome act of Calvary. And as though this central truth of a faith yet unrevealed had been momentarily glimpsed, the psalmist continues with his vision of a world turned Godwards.

**6–8** From the firm based mass of Hermon standing white-capped on the northern frontier to the wild lines of endless surf assailing the long beaches from Ashkelon to Carmel's tip, all nature spoke, as it must still speak to a reverent mind, of the might of the Intelligence behind creation.

**9–11** As Paul told the people of the remote country town of Lystra, God was evident in all nature. Before the spread of cities clogged the earth, men were more intimate with the world of natural things; the stars shone in unpolluted air, the rain and the sun were the source of comfort, food, all else. Man felt more a part of the world. The sun was watched from morning to twilight, the movements of its blazing orb an arch of praise across the sky. The Hebrew was too deep in his understanding to deify the sun and moon. He saw behind both and in them God's visitation of His earth. God comes enriching, not with empty hands.

**12,13** It is as though the bare land clothes itself 'like Solomon in all his glory', to welcome the divine guest. The mottling of flocks on far hillsides, the golden cloak of the ripe grain, the pale green veil over the bare wilderness, are the earth's rich mantle of welcome for the God of the harvest. The picture goes far beyond the fantasies of nature-worship.

### Conclusion

Many nations have built mythologies, sometimes crude, sometimes beautiful, around the thought of Heaven and Earth, united to produce their offspring. All manner of nature worship, cults of fertility, the adoration of the warming sun, find origin in this concept. The Hebrew hymn shows how magnificently more mature, how far more truly intelligent, was the faith in God's beneficence which one small nation had discovered. It is the unseen hand behind the bounty of the fields, the planning of a loving heart and mind, which preoccupy the psalmist. The whole world is gloriously alive, girding on its robe of green, waving its crops in song and praise, but never for a moment is the Creation confused with the Creator. The landscape is alive, adorned for harvest festival, but it is God the Giver who is praised, for whom adoration 'waits'. The Hebrew consciousness of divine beneficence does not issue in some myth of a resurrected Corn God, some Persephone coming back to earth to bring the summer, some cult of the Baal of the Field, to be aided in his insemination of the earth and watering of the grain by base rituals of promiscuity – but in such rich poetry as Wordsworth made:

*An intermingling of Heaven's pomp is spread*
*On ground which British shepherds tread . . .*

*One impulse from a vernal wood*
*May teach you more of man . . .*

*And I have felt*
*A presence that disturbs me with the joy*
*Of elevated thoughts – a sense sublime*
*Of something far more deeply interfused . . .*

*This City now doth like a garment wear*
*The beauty of the morning . . .*

*Everybody suddenly burst out singing . . .*

Of course did not the same Wordsworth say: 'Poetry is the breath and finer spirit of all knowledge, it is the impassioned expression which is in the countenance of all science'?

**Read Psalm 66; Isaiah 33**

**Occasion and author**

The writer is unknown. Echoes of words in the preceding psalm would seem to have suggested placing the composition in this place. The central section (8–12) speaks of a great deliverance from some fearsome menace and national testing. The historical events most likely to fit such a time would be the impact and passing of Sennacherib's invasion. More cannot be said.

**Commentary**

**1–4** The words seem to suggest some great occasion of festival or national jubilation with a vast congregation joining in a majestic hymn of praise. The land feels strong in God. The enemy cowers before the demonstration of His power (3, NEB). The notion of 'growing less' seems to be contained in the verb. 'Thine enemies dwindle away before Thee', runs a new Jewish

translation. What impresses is the sight not seen today – a nation tingling with confidence, not in itself, but in the One who has preserved them.
**5–7** His works are awesome. If this jubilant psalm can indeed be attached to the melting away (dwindling?) of the great Assyrian host, it was natural enough that a writer, richly conscious of history, should find a third deliverance to set beside the famous stories of the Red Sea and the Jordan. The perpetually beleaguered land is shown to have an ally which those who gaze greedily across the menaced frontiers might well consider in their plans.
**8–12** They live when they had feared to die, they stand when their foothold appeared to crumble underneath (9), they have passed the testing of the fire with purging of the dross (10). Those whose hearts in a reach of faith responded to Isaiah's call for confidence, might well feel that the great vindication they had seen had for ever changed their lives. They had felt trapped, and were free, bowed under the burdens of anxiety and stress, but were free, delivered (12). They had watched the rolling chariot wheels, and the thundering cavalry of a savage foe, and felt like the beaten earth and the dust they raised, but had been led out to liberty (Moffatt), a spacious place (RSV), prosperity (R. K. Harrison). The word is literally 'overflow', the word of Psa. 23.5. The 'fire and water' of the ordeal seem to echo Isaiah's wider promise (43.2).
**13–20** The psalm suddenly merges into a personal petition. Is it the king speaking personally in testimony? Is it so designed that each man can make the public prayer his own? In the latter thought lies the whole art of public prayer. He who chooses words for another's need must so choose that those who listen can appropriate and use the prayer he frames. At v. 16, if the king is speaking, the words become poignant for their humility. A clean heart could hardly speak with deeper simplicity and sincerer eloquence. In the closing verses, the psalmist touches a principle of prayer common to the Old Testament and the New. To 'cherish iniquity in the heart', in other words wilfully to entertain known sin, to live at peace with some evil thing, unopposed and unjudged, is to frustrate prayer.

If God demanded perfection in those who come to Him, none could come; but He does demand that we do battle with sin, confess it, and in His name endeavour to overcome it. 'God has truly heard me,' cries the psalmist in v. 19. He has not 'rejected' the suppliant's prayer nor hid His 'mercy' or 'steadfast love'. In His mercy He forgave acknowledged sin, and with the forgiveness His ear was open to the penitent's prayer.

Confession should be prayer's beginning. Those who come to God should search the heart and seek no paltry hiding-place for things offensive in His sight. Christ's righteousness can be ours (1 Cor. 1.30). Thus clothed we can approach our God.

## Conclusion

All the religion of the Old Testament is in this psalm. Here is God the great Creator, who demands righteousness and punishes iniquity, who blesses His people but judges their sin, the God whom men should revere, and yet who cares for those who seek Him, and answers their prayer. We can envy a people so united before God, and wistfully desire such returning among those of our own race. If such desire seems too elusive we can at least stand with the solitary suppliant and begin, where all revival must begin, with our own hearts.

**Read Psalm 67; Genesis 15.1–6; Numbers 6.22–27**

**Occasion and author**
The writer of the psalm is unknown. It was part of the Temple hymn-book, the product of an age of hope, perhaps following the days which saw Israel lie in an unaccustomed patch of peace. The little hymn is based on the benediction of Numbers 6. The priestly blessing was familiar language in the Temple, but the psalm adds a touch of the old Abrahamic blessing which widened its horizon to gather in all the peoples of the earth.

**Commentary**
**1–7** Observe that v. 3 is wrongly translated with a singular in the KJV and one or two other versions. The evangelical vision of a global faith is embedded in the Old Testament, and perceptive Jewish minds, even before the days of Christianity, recognized the wider mission of Israel. The dominant image is God's rich beneficence, bathing man and the world like the life-giving and comforting sun. But why? In order that those thus blessed may pass their blessing to others '... that thy way may be known upon earth, and thy saving power among all nations.' Note the words. God's will is a way of life, and Christianity at first bore this name (Acts 9.2).

The followers of Christ were 'the people of the Way' distinguished by the life they led, and the firm path of uprightness which they trod. 'Saving health' (KJV) can come to the world's sick nations only when the men and women who form them walk in such a way. How sadly does the world that is, contrast with the world that might be! 'Let the nations be glad and sing for joy,' cries the psalmist, and such joy God offers men.

It is man's choice of evil which has taken gladness from the world, and filled it with hate, jealousy, glowering resentment, crude self-assertion, pride and all the varied devilry of sin.

The message of v. 4 with its view of God as Judge and Guide adds a warm touch to the psalm. Man so easily sets a frown upon the face of God. Thomas of Celano, it is said, put the *Dies Irae* into the hymnology of the Church eight centuries ago – so lilting in its Latin, so grim in its meaning –

*Dies irae, dies illa*
*Solvent saeclum in favilla*
*Teste David cum Sibylla*

*Quantus tremor est futurus*
*Quando iudex est venturus*
*Cuncta stricte discussurus . . .*

And so on *crescendo* through eighteen stanzas.

*Day of wrath, Oh dreadful day,*
*In ashes pass the worlds away,*
*Both David and the Sibyl say . . .*

*What horror, horror then will be*
*When comes the Judge that is to see*
*Each thing that is unsparingly . . .*

The Hebrew concept of God the Shepherd, the Guide, the Being of 'loving-kindness' is unique and a concept scarcely to be held save in the light of the glory of Christ . . .

The psalm, a hymn in which, as Maclaren puts it, 'aspirations tremble on the edge of being prophecies', ends with renewed benediction.

**Read Psalm 68; 2 Samuel 6; Hebrews 12.18–24**

**Occasion and author**

Both Kidner and Maclaren comment on the rush and vigour of the language in this national anthem. It was some high occasion and could be a composition of David to celebrate the bearing of the Ark from the house of Obed-Edom to Jerusalem. The formal words connected with the beautiful symbol of the land's devotion inspire the opening words (Num. 10.35). The reference to the events of Sinai and the wilderness, to the marching choirs, to the hill of God, seem to support the placing of the psalm in this background.

**Commentary**

**1–6** 'God arises and his enemies are scattered' (NEB) is probably the best translation. It is a reach of faith rather than a prayer for divine intervention.

That the ancient object should at that moment be carried high and gleaming by the bearers, followed by the colourful procession, implied that the frontiers were still. It was an occasion for good men to be joyful and glad. It is worth remembering that the Phoenician Storm God, Baal, had 'Rider on the Clouds' as one of his titles (4). And then, after dismissing the violent deity of paganism, the theme turns to what the nation, alone among all nations of the world, conceived their Lord to be, the giver of comfort, justice, liberty, the blessings of peace. The desert was the land of those who denied Him their allegiance (6) and, indeed, beyond Israel's borders to this day, the hostile Arab and his foes have always been the children of the sand, the drought, and the wilderness. '*Solitudinem faciunt pacem appellant,*' said a British chief described by Tacitus: 'They make a desert and they call it peace.' The words were true of many an ancient empire.

**7–10** It was like another Exodus with God before a marching host, nature itself, from the gaunt mass of Sinai to the healing rains, seeming to unite with man to praise God. It is a peculiar facet of deep happiness to feel this communion of natural things, a spiritual experience too often denied the modern denizens of an urbanized world. The wilderness, in all Hebrew thought, was the place of the presence of God, the city the thing of man. And history, too, was to them the demonstration of His purposes, the guarantee of all those qualities listed in vs. 5,6.

**11–16** In v. 8 there was an echo of Deborah's song and perhaps of the violent storm which disconcerted Sisera (Judg. 5). The echoes continue (4,5,13,16) as though the old lyric was still alive in the psalmist's mind. Verses 13, 14 contain a difficult allusion variously explained. 'Pots' (KJV) or 'sheepfolds' (RSV, NEB)? The gilded and silver dove? What? The whiteness of Zalmon? With snow? With the scattered debris of battle? It is impossible to say. Some local or contemporary fragment of information is wanting. The wonder is that poetry so ancient does not contain more obscurities. Nor does it diminish the stature of a commentator to admit that there is no clear indication of what the writer had in mind.

It may be interesting to mention H. C. Leopold's suggestion. He translates: 'Will you lie among the sheepfolds? – Wings of a dove covered with silver and its pinions with yellow gold. When the Almighty scattered kings there, snow fell on the Black Mountain.' The first half of the verse, says Leopold, 'is a rebuke for those who, like Reuben, withdrew their aid. The second part is a description of some notable item of beauty (the missing factor mentioned above) . . .' Verse 14 may refer to a scene on the battlefield – a hillside, like Ezekiel's valley plain (*beqaa*) where he saw the vision of the slain, some relic of a rearguard action as Nebuchadnezzar drove down through Palestine. Albright suggests that Zalmon, the 'Black Mountain', may be Jebel Druse on the borders of Bashan. Does Druse suggest the mightier Hermon which is not a single summit, but a range? The obscurity which haunts the middle section of this allusive psalm continues. The great proud peaks are bidden not to 'look askance' (Leopold), 'look with envy' (RSV), 'look down on' (JB), 'look jealously' (NASB), on little Zion. Greatness, in any sphere, is not dependent upon size. Consider what a land the size of Wales, Sicily, the State of Vermont, has given the world. And it was Isaac Watts who said:

*Were I so tall to reach the Pole*
*Or grasp the ocean in my span,*
*I must be measured by my soul –*
*The mind's the standard of the man.*

**17,18** The correct rendering of this further difficult verse seems to be that of A. Weiser, who translates the last clause: 'the Lord is with them, Sinai is in the holy place.' This forcefully implies that where God is, there is Sinai, the law, the commandments, and all that the place of God's visitation signifies. Zion, Sinai, Hermon, might be geographical symbols of God's presence, action, encounter. In fact, He is never far away. 'Where Jesus is it's Heaven there' – He walks on any lake, speaks on the shore of all our days, commands in thunder on any eminence of life. Derek Kidner, who develops this thought in a perceptive note, quotes aptly Heb. 12.18–24.

Having thus established Zion as a symbol of God's indwelling, the song of the processional hymn continues. With echoes again of Deborah's victory song and continuing reference to a new exodus, the ark goes up to the city as in Psa. 24. We need not be too prosaic over the captives and the tributes. Let us keep the old fine translation which Paul carried one step higher in symbolism (Eph. 4.8). It was as though the horror of captivity itself was carried chained in the bright procession, never more to stalk and pounce. This is a poem.

**19–23** The moving procession suggests a day of victory and if the imagery seems to Christian readers somewhat violent (e.g. 23) the anxieties of a land ringed by violent enemies ready to soak their tilth in blood must be remembered. The Assyrians' 'black bearded kings with wolflike eyes', with heavy heads of hair, are familiar from their own monuments. Assyria had not yet risen to curse the Middle East when David wrote these words, but the image of v. 21 was a familiar picture of fear. Here, in the host moving towards the ark's resting place in Zion, was the demonstration of a new peace, frontiers secured, savage foes cast back.

**24–27** The procession itself 'comes into view'. From poetic symbolism the theme turns to reality, as though from some vantage point the psalmist is watching intently for the host to appear marching to Zion. All Israel is on the march.

**28–31** The reality of the scene fades in a vision of coming peace and the rebuke of vast evil empires. It is a vision such as Isaiah had in the majestic closing chapters of his great book (e.g. 60). Verse 30 has challenged the translators as well as the commentators. RSV makes sense: 'Rebuke the beasts that dwell among the reeds (that is, Egypt with its great papyrus swamps), the herd of bulls with the calves of the peoples (that is, the powerful brutes which lead docile peoples to aggression). Trample under foot those who lust after tribute (for example, though from a later age, Isa. 10.13), and scatter the peoples who delight in war.' An Israeli might quote the words today.

**32–35** Simply read these verses as a crashing fanfare. The ark stands where it was to stand, and in a wild crescendo of song the hymn and the procession end.

**Read Psalm 69; Matthew 27.25–30; Romans 11.9,10**

**Occasion and author**

It is seldom that clues are lacking concerning the reason for the placing of a psalm. Some sequence of mood, identity of historical background, or clear echoes of language and imagery, generally supply some reason why a certain order is observed. The only reason which suggests itself lies in the title. The psalm is attributed to David, and more than once we have expressed respect for an inscription which is ancient and traditional. Could it be that the editor, with the end of two books predominantly Davidic in view, and having already decided to end with a psalm attributed to Solomon, thought it proper to break the sequence of national and patriotic hymns by a prayer typical of the chief psalmist's darker moods?

The only competitor for the authorship, if tradition is to be discarded, is Jeremiah. Those who take this line refer to passages in the prophet's pages, like 9.18ff; 12.1ff; 15.10ff; 17.12ff; 18.18ff; 20.7ff. It would not detract from the power, and the authenticity of the psalm if two great poets had a part in it. Suppose a psalm basically Davidic meant much in Jeremiah's personal experience, and suppose a version survived with the prophet's experience interwoven with that of the royal psalmist?

The psalm has been described as messianic. That term can be too loosely held, for the author of this prayer is deeply conscious of his sin and also uses language which is quite unlike that of Christ. Say rather that it is quoted in the New Testament more frequently than any psalm other than the twenty-second. Events in the Gospels remind the apostles of familiar words from a book they had no doubt had by heart (e.g. Matt. 27.27–30, 34; John 2.17; 15.25; 19.28. Also Acts 1.20; Rom. 11.9,10). This is not to say that the psalm is directly prophetic. As with Psa. 22, the writer, in the fervour of his committal to God of his agony and aspiration, breaks a barrier of time and finds his mind and speech merging with the eternal.

**Commentary**

**1–4; 13–15** 'The waters have come up to my neck' (RSV). The figure has puzzled translators. It is notable that, apart from the vivid word-picture in Psa. 69, there is little said of mud in the Bible. Palestine was a dry land for most of the year, and when rain fell the near-tropic sun rapidly dried out the soil. The KJV avoids the word 'mud', and uses 'mire' for the unpleasant thing. In only three or four places do the modern versions risk a change. Job speaks of the mud in which the great papyrus sedge grows (8.11), and of mud as a symbol of the chill contempt into which his stricken life was cast (30.19). Isaiah uses the mud of the winter street as a figure for the rejected rebel trodden under foot by the Assyrians' mailed feet (10.6), a picture repeated by Zechariah (9.3) writing of the silver and gold of Tyre. And in one of the rare sea pictures of the Old Testament, Isaiah likens the jetsam of the waves, beating the beach after a night of storm, to the refuse tossed from the restless hearts of wicked men.

But to return to Psa. 69. 'Save me, O God,' cries the psalmist, 'for the waters are come in unto my soul. I sink in deep mire where there is no standing. I am come into deep waters where the floods overflow me' (1,2). He returns to the image in vs. 14,15: 'Deliver me out of the mire. Let me be delivered from them that hate me and out of the deep waters. Let not the waterflood overflow me, neither let the deep swallow me up, and let not the pit shut her mouth upon me.'

The modern translators are rather at a loss over the passage. The Jerusalem Bible pictures such a swamp. 'I am sinking in the deepest swamp, there is no foothold and the waves are washing over me . . . Pull me out of the swamp, let me sink no further. Do not let the waves wash over me, do not let the deep swallow me, or the Pit close its mouth over me.' The Pit, it is to be noticed, is here Sheol or death. The NEB pictures the suppliant trying to ford a river in spate, the Jordan, perhaps, though that river was a cleaner, stonier stream before the silt of the long valley had built its yellow mass at the Dead Sea end. It runs: 'Save me, O God, for the waters have risen up to my neck. I sink in muddy depths and have no foothold. I am swept into deep water, and the flood carries me away . . . Rescue me from the mire. Do not let me sink. Let me be rescued from the muddy depths so that no flood may carry me away, no abyss swallow me up, no deep close over me.'

Knox 'halts between two opinions', drowning in the ocean, drowning in a well: 'O God, save me. See how the waters close about me, shoulder-high! I am like one who sticks fast in deep mire with no ground under his feet, one who has ventured out into mid-ocean to be drowned in the storm . . . Save me from sinking in the mire, rescue me from my enemies, from the deep waters that surround me. Let me not sink under the flood, swallowed up in its depths, and the well's mouth close over me.'

The sum of the meaning is that the encompassing, man-made evil is all but triumphant. It is a picture of distress which could hardly be more powerful.

**5–12** The psalmist admits the contribution which his own sin and folly had made and in battling with any evil situation it is well first to have done with that which has provoked the trial. There is sometimes confession, expiation, restitution to be made. God will still aid but He will hardly aid until we have faced our desperation and had done with sin.

The psalmist was jealous of God's honour. He had done his part and taken his stand on God's righteousness. The fact that echoes of these verses were considered messianic and phrases applied to Christ Himself, does not do away with an immediate meaning. David had sinned and suffered the humiliation of public penance. There were those like Shimei who still bayed for blood. It is obvious that the whole passage cannot prefigure the Lord.

Here is a man who has known the shame of exposure and the pain of confession. He has done his part and in simplicity of faith awaits God's salvation.

**16–21** The passage echoes Psa. 51 and the significance of this is obvious. The poignancy of vs. 17,18 reveals the depth and glory of the Hebrew understanding of God, and he is fortunate who has never been driven to this cry of anguish. Or is he fortunate? In such valleys of death's shadow man learns to know his God – words easier to write than weave into the fabric of faith's experience. 'Shame, reproach and dishonour' are the most difficult of life's agonies to bear. And yet – 'He bore the shame and scoffing rude, when in my place condemned He stood . . .' One can say little more on these verses without the sense of treading on holy ground. But learn v. 17 by heart. It could provide words when the heart and mind are too numb to discover any.

**22–28** It is tempting to wish that the psalm had ended with the last section, but this is the Old Testament and 'grace and truth', God's full revelation, came, as John said (1.17), with Jesus Christ. Can we say that these words are in the text of Scripture by God's permission? There will be occasion in a later psalm to discuss one purpose of the imprecatory passages which is sometimes overlooked. A curse could be a weapon; living, barbed words which fought for the victim; haunted, hunted and pursued the persecutors; and had a protective function. Thus included in the psalm they are a demonstration of a stage in the progress of revelation. David cries for justice, and that is a prime function of the Old Testament. Cruelty is a loathsome thing. The withholding of compassion from one who has suffered under judgement is a sign of the last baseness of man. No one can view callous persecution with a cool mind if he cares, feels, suffers with the suffering. These people, swept by the wind of this language, were those who sneered and mocked before the cross of Christ. The world is weary of them.

**29–36** The last eight verses form a psalm by themselves. The humble, the poor and the sorrowful are upheld before God. The Beatitudes similarly uphold them.

# 70

These five verses are from Psa. 40 with some insignificant changes. They form the last five verses of the earlier psalm which, curiously, occupies a similar penultimate position in Book One of the Psalter. The reason why they were detached from the earlier passage is not apparent. Perhaps some liturgical purpose was in view. Perhaps they form a conclusion and a summary of the preceding psalm and round off its theme. We cannot tell.

**Read Psalm 71; 1 John 2**

### Occasion and author

No author is mentioned, but the writer, or perhaps the compiler, uses Davidic expressions as the most cursory reading will show. The writer appears to be old, to have known the power of his God, and to call upon it as his strength wanes. The author knew well Pss. 22,31,35,40. Jeremiah is named as a possible author on the grounds of subject and style. One can well imagine that Jeremiah would know well the Davidic psalms and might, in such a prayer, skilfully fuse no fewer than ten quotations from the Psalter. Such is a function of memorized Scripture – to provide speech when speech fails.

### Commentary

**1–3** These verses almost reproduce the opening of Psa. 31. The intrusion of the word 'continually' (3, KJV) is a touch of pathos. The ageing man clings to the hope that all will be well to the end.

**4–7** Note 'continually' again in the prayer. What sort of 'wonder' the suppliant has in mind is not clear – probably the word refers to his continuing years. He knows their fragility and trusts that what has been will be. In an environment ever more lonely, with strength failing, he has only one refuge. Who was it who remarked that 'it is not the beginning of a matter but the ending thereof that bringeth the true glory'?

**8–14** Friends grow fewer as the years take their toll but for some enemies multiply. The psalmist seems to have held some prominent position and there were those eager to see him gone. 'Continually', he says again (14).

**15–18** There is work for the old to do. John wrote his Gospel in his nineties. The Venerable Bede translated it into English as he lay dying. It is true that the arteries harden and the mind stiffens in mortal man, but it is also true that the Spirit of God is not constricted and that the willing heart can be enlightened at any age, illumined anew and delighted with fresh revelation. Nor need usefulness cease (1 John 2.7,8). Memorize v. 18 – it may one day be useful.

**19–24** William Ernest Henley wrote tenderer words than his arrogant *Invictus*. Hear him in more Christian lines:

*So be my passing*
*My task accomplished and the long day done,*
*My wages taken, and in my heart*
*Some late lark singing . . .*

The psalm is ending with much gentleness, with praise for a plan revealed, for mercy known, for comfort given. 'That unhoped serene which men call age', of which young Rupert Brooke dreamed, can be life's most tranquil evening. It calls for courage, as Tennyson's magnificent Ulysses said:

*Tho' much is taken, much abides; and tho'*
*We are not now that strength which in old days*
*Moved earth and heaven; that which we are, we are;*
*One equal temper of heroic hearts,*
*Made weak by time and fate, but strong in will*
*To strive, to seek, to find and not to yield.*

Note the last line.

# 72

**Read Psalm 72; Matthew 5.1–10**

**Occasion and author**

If the common rendering of the Hebrew in the inscriptions to the Psalms is consistently followed, this is a 'Psalm of Solomon' (RSV), not a 'Psalm for Solomon' (KJV), grammatically possible though the rendering would be. Calvin suggested that it was both – a psalm of David for his son, worked over and appropriated by Solomon for an anthem in his day. It is a fine piece of poetry, the base of more than one hymn – for example, 'Jesus shall reign where'er the sun . . .'

**Commentary**

**1–4** Righteousness and justice are the ruler's supreme virtues. The Hebrew passion for justice, especially, dominates every notion of sound authority in the Old Testament. And is that not always the case? If corruption sits enthroned in high places it inevitably filters down through all levels of society. It is 'the poor' (2, 4) who long most for this benediction.

Sir George Adam Smith, in his great study on Isa. 25, writes movingly on the theme. 'The poor' were a common theme with Isaiah. Read the beautiful fourth and eighth verses of the chapter, follow it through to 61.1 in the same book, and on seven centuries to the Capernaum synagogue (Luke 4.17,18). Smith pointed out that in the East poverty meant more than mere physical disadvantage. The poor man was, in popular religion, considered the God-forsaken, thought to lie under Heaven's frown, deprived because he merited deprivation. And commonly this is what he himself believed. It was, at least, his daily humiliating, despairing doubt. It thus came about that the poor man was reft of justice, respect, acceptance, the butt of common scorn and ill-treatment. He was lonely, burdened in heart – in a word, 'poor in spirit', for his poverty seeped into all his thoughts and feelings, corrupting heart and mind. He hungered, therefore, for God, for justice, for love, as well as for his daily food. And, says the commentator, 'it was by developing, with the aid of God's Spirit, this quick conscience, and this deep desire for God, which in the East are the very soul of physical poverty, that the Jews advanced to the sense of evangelical poverty of heart, blessed by Jesus in the first of His Beatitudes, as the possession of the Kingdom of Heaven.' The 'Kingdom of Heaven' means, after all, the royal rule of God, or, if you will, 'the Lordship of Christ'. The proud and the self-sufficient can never know it, and the first temptation and peril of wealth is precisely the self-confidence which corrupts and the arrogant self-esteem which damns.

'Peace' (3), the lovely Hebrew word *shalom,* means also prosperity. Hence RSV and NEB 'peace and prosperity'.

**5,6** Say 'revere' rather than fear. The readings of the RSV, NEB and other modern translations reflect a slightly different Hebrew text which possibly lies behind the LXX which they follow. Reverence implies respect for authority, and without authority in high places, order beneath, as the world knows, collapses (5). The beautiful metaphor of the rain shows that fear is not terror (6). Like Shakespeare's mercy, the good king's beneficence droppeth as the gentle rain from heaven'.

**7–19** It follows that, if such a ruler is enthroned, time and space for his dominion have no limits in the desires of good men. This is why the emperor Augustus was revered. He brought peace to a world long torn with strife and some of the most majestic of Latin poetry praised his rule. And it was while Augustus gave the old world peace that One was born whom some find foreshadowed in this hymn of the great Solomon.

'From sea to sea' (8) meant from the Mediterranean surf to the Indian Ocean, the Persian Gulf and the Red Sea. The desert dwellers, Palestine's old menace, dwelt in the great Arabian wilderness (9, KJV). Tarshish was Tartessus in Spain to which Solomon's ore ships ('ships of Tarshish') sailed in partnership with the seafarers of Tyre and Sidon. And the ships of Tarshish also sailed out of the Gulf of Aqaba to Ophir where Sheba met Israel, and to the Malabar Coast whence came their 'ivory and apes and peacocks'. Gold came from Ophir in Southern Arabia, by ship up the Red Sea or along the incense routes by which Sheba's queen travelled.

Verse 16 is cleared up in modern versions. RSV has a smooth rendering and Moffatt a fine poetic turn: 'May the land be rich in waving corn, right up to the top of the hills! May the folk flourish like trees in Lebanon, may citizens flower like grass in the field!'

The benediction follows . . .

**Conclusion**

Verse 20 sets a name to the first two books of the Psalms. Perhaps an earlier collection comprised only the Psalms of David and the title was retained when the collection was expanded to equal the other books. David will appear again but the collection to this point has been a deeply moving experience of intimacy with a great poet's soul in his joys, sorrows, elation and despair.